See You In Bells

A Comedy in Three Acts

by Edie Claire

Single copies of plays are sold for reading purposes only. The copying or duplicating of a play, or any part of play, by hand or by any other process, is an infringement of the copyright. Such infringement will be vigorously prosecuted

Baker's Plays
7611 Sunset Blvd.
Los Angeles, CA 90042
bakersplays.com

NOTICE

This book is offered for sale at the price quoted only on the understanding that, if any additional copies of the whole or any part are necessary for its production, such additional copies will be purchased. The attention of all purchasers is directed to the following: This work is protected under the copyright laws of the United States of America, in the British Empire, including the Dominion of Canada, and all other countries adhering to the Universal Copyright Convention. Violations of the Copyright Law are punishable by fine or imprisonment, or both. The copying or duplication of this work or any part of this work, by hand or by any process, is an infringement of the copyright and will be vigorously prosecuted.

This play may not be produced by amateurs or professionals for public or private performance without first submitting application for performing rights. Royalties are due on all performances whether for charity or gain, or whether admission is charged or not. Since performance of this play without the payment of the royalty fee renders anybody participating liable to severe penalties imposed by the law, anybody acting in this play should be sure, before doing so, that the royalty fee has been paid. Professional rights, reading rights, radio broadcasting, television and all mechanical rights, etc. are strictly reserved. Application for performing rights should be made directly to BAKER'S PLAYS.

No one shall commit or authorize any act or omission by which the copyright of, or the right to copyright, this play may be impaired. No one shall make any changes in this play for the purpose of production.

Publication of this play does not imply availability for performance. Both amateurs and professionals considering a production are strongly advised in their own interest to apply to Baker's Plays for written permission before starting rehearsals, advertising, or booking a theatre.

Whenever the play is produced, the author's name must be carried in all publicity, advertising and programs. Also, the following notice must appear on all printed programs, "Produced by special arrangement with Baker's Plays."

Licensing fees for *SEE YOU IN BELLS* is based on a per performance rate and payable one week in advance of the production.

Please consult the Baker's Plays website at www.bakersplays.com or our current print catalogue for up to date licensing fee information.

Copyright © 2008 by Edie Claire
Made in U.S.A.
All rights reserved.

SEE YOU IN BELLS
ISBN 978-0-87440-312-1
#1828-B

CHARACTERS

DICK BOWER, MD, Father of the Bride (60ish)*** A devoted father and husband, but the women in his life drive him nuts

BARBARA BOWER, Mother of the Bride (60ish)*** A born worrier, all she wants is for everything to be perfect, and for no one to be hospitalized

BRIAN BOWER, Brother of the Bride (early 40s)*** The longsuffering peacemaker of the family, he'll risk anything to stop his sisters' feud—including hospitalization

DEB BOWER, Sister of the Bride (early 40s)*** A successful, career-driven, take-no-prisoners businesswoman who HAS NO SISTER other than the bride

CAT BOWER, Sister of the Bride (early 40s)*** A willful, mischievous, and sometimes irrational free spirit who is strangely unrepentant at ruining Deb's entire life

JENNA BOWER, The Bride (mid-late 20s)** The beloved baby of the family whom everyone wants to protect, and whom everyone underestimates

SCOTT SANDERS, The Groom (mid-late 20s)** Honest and patient, he can tolerate any number of insane in-laws, but would prefer to skip straight to the honeymoon

NADINE APPLEBY, Wedding Coordinator (60ish)*** Barb's longtime friend, she is quirky, sentimental, devoted, meddlesome…and just a tad bit malicious

PAUL MYERS, Best Man (late 30s/early 40s)** Uncle of the groom, he is intelligent, witty, dryly sarcastic and—unlike everyone else—not intimidated by Deb

JIM SANDERS, Father of the Groom (50ish)* He just wants to get back to his workshop—and away from Dolores

DOLORES SANDERS, Mother of the Groom (50ish)* She LOVES weddings, and thinks Jim should too

YOUNG BRIAN, A flashback to the late 70s/early 80s (teenager)**

YOUNG DEB, A flashback to the late 70s/early 80s (teenager)**

YOUNG CAT, A flashback to the late 70s/early 80s (teenager)**

KEVIN STILLS, Deb's erstwhile fiancé, a.k.a. pond scum (40ish)*

THE MINISTER, non-speaking cameo in the Finale*

*** Lead Roles
 ** Supporting Roles
  * Opportunities with lesser time commitment

Premiere Performances October 25-27, 2007
"Acts of God" Drama Ministry
Ingomar United Methodist Church

Directed by Kim Gibson

Original Cast

BARBARA	Carolyn Tornow
DICK	Tom Roush
BRIAN	Rick Mitchell
DEB	Jan Barber
CAT	Edie Claire
JENNA	Mollie Brooks
NADINE	Carol Wiltman
SCOTT	Sam Rosenhamer
PAUL	Ralph Karsh
DOLORES	Trina Walker
JIM	Hank Lawhead
YOUNG DEB	Lauren Barber
YOUNG BRIAN	Luke Gibson
YOUNG CAT	Julie Henderson
KEVIN	Mark Swihart

Check out more plays and novels by Edie Claire at www.edieclaire.com!

SETTING

The present, in any church sanctuary, anywhere in the country, any time of year.

PRODUCTION NOTES

See You in Bells was written specifically for churches with plenty of dramatic talent and enthusiasm…but not so big a budget. The show is designed at every turn to be flexible to stage, simple to pull together, inexpensive to produce, and incredibly fun to perform!

STAGING

Minimal requirements are that the sanctuary have one forward exit stage left and one rear exit, with some means of communication between the two. (Running around outside the building in the rain will work just fine.) Two forward exits on either side of the chancel are ideal, but a "captive" exit—existing or created—will suffice for stage right, and with some creative staging, it is possible to dispense with stage right altogether.

SET DESIGN

The Bower's beloved church building is very old, in bad shape structurally, and due to be demolished, but your church need not be in disrepair to play the part. With the audience viewing the sanctuary through the actors' eyes, strategic placement of a few drop cloths, rain buckets, and mops is all that will be necessary to create an effective illusion. Stock wedding decorations, tasteful or otherwise, will add to the visuals in Acts II and III.

COSTUMES

Adult actors wear whatever their characters might ordinarily wear to a wedding rehearsal dinner, and then to a wedding. For men in the wedding party, begged or borrowed tuxedos will look sharp, but are optional. If an already-seen-better-days wedding dress for the bride is difficult to locate, a layer of netting stained with brown paint and covered with dead leaves can be pinned onto a dress no one wants to injure. As for finding vintage 80s-style clothes to force the teens to wear…well, that's just plain fun.

PROPS

A wheelchair, a set of crutches, a box of ribbons and bows, one big piece of unstained plywood, two acolyte candle-lighters, and some cellular phones will do it.

LIGHTING

At a minimum, two handheld spots are necessary for the flashback scenes, in addition to adequate lighting in the chancel area (preferably, at least two different levels).

Dedicated to the memory of Betty Snow and Daniel R. Mitchell, Jr.

ACT ONE

(Dim, low-level lighting illuminates the chancel area. A door creaks offstage. [The creaking noise is attributed to an unseen door in a vestibule just outside the stage left entrance. The sound precedes and follows all entrances/ exits from stage left throughout the play. Precise timing, where critical, is noted.] In a few seconds, **BARBARA** *rushes in stage left, flicking switches on the wall.)*

BARBARA. The bulb's not burned out, Dick! The lights in the sanctuary are off, too! Oh, I just *knew* something like this would happen – and now of all times!

DICK *(offstage)* It'll be all right, Barbara. Calm down.

BARBARA. I will *not* calm down until this whole thing is over and my little girl is happily married. I just knew we were tempting fate, having the ceremony here! The power's probably down all over the building – it'll take *days* to fix –

DICK *(offstage)* I'm sure it's just a blown circuit...happens all the time. I'll go down and flip the breaker – just sit tight.

BARBARA. *(paces, mutters to herself)* Sit tight! Easy for him to say. He doesn't believe in curses. No matter how many Bower family weddings have gone up in flames! Don't be silly, Barb! It's all just a bunch of coincidences, Barb! Just because every single religious ceremony associated with the Bower family in the last seventy years has resulted in some sort of disaster is *no reason* to be worried! Everything will be FINE.

*(***BRIAN*** enters through the rear entrance.)*

BRIAN. Hey, Mom. I didn't know you were here. Listen, I just tried to turn on the lights in the narthex –

(**BARBARA** *comes partway down the aisle to meet him.*)

BARBARA. They're down. The whole circuit's blown again. It's a sign. I knew it. We should have told your sister to go to the Justice of the Peace and be done with it!

BRIAN. Mom, will you knock that off? Everything's going to be fine.

BARBARA. Says your father.

BRIAN. Well, he's right. You and Jenna are both being silly. There is no curse, and this wedding *will* be everything she's always dreamed of. I promise.

(*He throws a comforting arm around* **BARBARA**; *they move to chancel.*)

BARBARA. I wish I could believe that. I really do. Jenna's such a wonderful girl – she deserves to be happy. And I know she will be, with Scott. It's not the *marriage* that worries me – our family has a pretty good track record with those. But the weddings…that's another matter. And you know what it is that Jenna *really* wants tomorrow…

BRIAN. Yes, I know.

BARBARA. Well, what can any of us do about *that*? Your sisters are like two cats in a bag!

BRIAN. Two *rabid* cats.

BARBARA. Then how can you stand here and say that everything's going to go all right?!

(*Full lighting comes up over the sanctuary.* **BRIAN** *raises his hands.*)

BRIAN. What can I say, Mom? I believe in miracles.

(**NADINE**, *the wedding coordinator, bursts in rear entrance. She is carrying stacks of ribbons, bows, fake flowers, etc. in complete disarray. The ribbons are wrapped around her and she is tripping over them as she comes forward.*)

NADINE. Barbara, dear, there you are! I've got all the flowers ready to go up front, you just need to take a quick look – I'd be *hours* ahead by now but I had to get just the right ribbon and they were all out of the frost so I had to get the lilac and then when I was in the storeroom looking for twine all the lights went out again and I nearly fell and busted my –

(She erupts into nervous laughter.)

Oh, I LOVE weddings!

BARBARA. Yes. We know.

NADINE. Well, this is going to be SUCH a special one! Your baby girl! Beating both her big sisters to the altar – who would have guessed? It's going to be *perfect*, Barbara, just perfect. And to think it will be the *last* wedding ever held in this old sanctuary!

(She looks around, gets choked up.)

Oh, can you believe they want to tear this beautiful old place down?

*(**DICK** enters stage left as **NADINE** walks up onto the chancel. She flips on a light switch and an additional area of the chancel lights up briefly, but then an ominous buzzing noise sounds, and the rest of the sanctuary lights flicker and go off again.)*

DICK. Gosh darnit!

(He whirls around and heads back off stage left.)

NADINE. Well, I suppose the building does have it problems. But then again, don't we all?

*(She attempts to cross the chancel toward stage right but, still wrapped up in ribbons, she trips and just catches herself from a spectacular fall. **BRIAN** steps forward, but she laughs and waves him away.)*

Oh, now don't you two worry about me! I'll have this place all beautified in no time, just like I always do. You know I've been doing this sort of thing practically all my life, and we've never lost a bride yet.

(She pauses.)

Not even at a Bower wedding!

(She ducks off hastily, stage right.)

BARBARA. See there?! Everybody knows! They're all just waiting for something horrible to happen.

BRIAN. Mom, my wedding went fine, remember?

BARBARA. But you didn't get married *here*. And besides, back then, your sisters were at least still speaking to each other. They haven't even been in the same room for *six years* now!

NADINE. *(pops her head out, stage right)* Six years! Has it really been that long since…well, since…that "other" wedding –

BARBARA. Nadine!

NADINE. I'm so sorry. I mean "the event that shall never be spoken of."

BARBARA. Yes, it's been six years. And we're *still* not speaking of it!

NADINE. Oh no, of course not. Never mind me…

*(**NADINE** ducks away again. The sanctuary lights come back on. **BRIAN** and **BARBARA** move away from stage right a little, where they can't be overheard.)*

BRIAN. And you're letting her coordinate this wedding why?

BARBARA. She comes with the sanctuary. Besides, we've been friends since before you were born, and if I cut her out of this she'd never speak to me again. And as disorganized as she is, she always does manage to pull everything together in the end. Virginia Smith's daughter's wedding was absolutely *perfect*.

BRIAN. Jenna's wedding will be too. I told you I'd take care of it.

BARBARA. You always were the peacemaker of the family. I still can't believe you got both your sisters to agree to come!

*(We hear a loud crash. **BARBARA** and **BRIAN** cringe.*

NADINE *enters stage right, looking disheveled.)*

NADINE. Um, Barb, honey? You got a minute?

*(***BARBARA** *takes off after* **NADINE**, *and the two exit stage right just as* **DICK** *enters stage left.)*

DICK. Hello there, Brian!

BRIAN. Hey, Dad. How are you holding up?

DICK. Oh, I'm the least of anyone's worries. It's your mother that needs a sedative. What was that crash?

BRIAN. Nadine.

DICK. Oh. Right.

(He looks around, making sure **BARBARA** *isn't within earshot.)*

Listen, son, I can't thank you enough for working things out with your sisters. It means the world to your mother that they're both going to come. We don't know how you did it…she's been trying for years to get those two talking again – neither one of us could budge them an inch.

BRIAN. *(suddenly uncomfortable)* Yeah, well, Dad, I've been meaning to tell you –

DICK. Never in my life have I seen two sisters bicker like them. From the time they were toddling around they were pulling each other's pigtails. But still, that was just bickering. The way they are now – this silence – it's not right. Ever since…since….

BRIAN. The event that shall never be spoken of.

DICK. Yes. Ever since *that*, well, nothing in this family's been right. It's hard enough to get Catherine out of the bush and back into the U.S.A. – but getting Deborah to the same place at the same time? I just wish I knew how you managed it.

BRIAN. No, Dad. You don't.

DICK. *(He pauses; looks at his son suspiciously.)* Brian?

BRIAN. Yes?

DICK. Deborah *does* know that Cat is coming. Doesn't she?

(BRIAN smiles sheepishly.)

DICK. *(slaps forehead)* Aw, son! Now *I'm* going to need a sedative!

BRIAN. It'll be okay, Dad! I've got it all worked out. I'm going to meet with both of them before the rehearsal dinner starts. All you have to do is get Mom out of here...we'll all meet you later at the banquet hall. We may be a little late, but we'll be there. All three of us.

DICK. In how many pieces?

(BARBARA and NADINE reenter stage right, talking as they come.)

NADINE. Well, I can understand Jenna's reasoning, I suppose, but still – this will be the first wedding I've ever done with only two attendants.

BARBARA. Trust me, it will be better this way. Jenna and Diane have been friends since grade school, and Scott's very close to his uncle. Besides, Deborah wouldn't be caught dead wearing taffeta, not since she hit 35...

NADINE. *(sing-song)* Always a bridesmaid, never a –

BARBARA. *Nadine!*

NADINE. Oh! Sorry, dear. I'll just get back to decorating...

(BRIAN gives DICK a meaningful nudge.)

DICK. Oh, right.

(to BARBARA, looking at watch)

Um, Barb, if you've checked whatever you were going to check, shouldn't we get back home and change? You said you wanted to get to the banquet hall a little early...

BARBARA. Oh, yes, and we've got to pick up those gifts.

(DICK leads BARBARA toward the stage left exit, BRIAN pushes her in the same direction. NADINE heads back down the aisle towards RE, eavesdropping as she goes.)

BARBARA. *(to BRIAN)* Are you sure Cat will make it here in time for the dinner?

BRIAN. I told her no later than three o'clock. It's five now. She should be here any minute.

BARBARA. Oh, I hope so!

*(She stops, becomes teary, gives **BRIAN** a hug.)*

Oh, Brian, honey, I'm so proud of you for working things out with your sisters. It means so much to Jenna...and to us.

BRIAN. *(uncomfortably)* Thanks, Mom. I know. See you later!

*(**DICK** hustles **BARBARA** off stage left. **NADINE** exits rear exit. **BRIAN** walks back to center, looks around, paces. Once alone, his confident air disappears.)*

BRIAN. *(looks heavenward)* Um...God? A little help here? I know I'm probably way overdue for a slapdown about... how shall I put it...making promises I can't possibly keep? But I was hoping, just this once, you could cut me a little slack and let it work? Please?

*(A door creaks. **BRIAN** looks toward stage left expectantly, and **CAT** bursts through the door at a run. She is wearing a free-flowing African-looking garment. Upon spying **BRIAN**, she shrieks and practically jumps into his arms.)*

BRIAN. *(with genuine affection)* Cat!

CAT. How are you? You look great! I can't believe it's been so long since we've seen each other. You *never* come to visit me!

BRIAN. Yes, well, I have a thing about malaria. And I'm kind of partial to flush toilets. Great invention, there.

*(**CAT** smacks **BRIAN** playfully on the shoulder.)*

CAT. Oh, don't be such a wimp. Our compound has its own well now, thank you very much. No more trips to the river for me.

(She moves around the chancel, studying the sanctuary.)

Oh, Brian...our little Jenna, getting married. Can you believe it?

BRIAN. Well, she couldn't stay a baby forever.

CAT. I wished she would! Remember when Mom found out she was pregnant again? And the three of us already teenagers! I remember Dad trying to pick her up off the floor.

BRIAN. I remember trying to pick Dad up off the floor.

CAT. But we were all thrilled, once we got used to the idea, weren't we? Poor Jenna, she was like the family pet!

BRIAN. She still is, in some ways.

(a pause)

And we all want to make sure this wedding is everything she's dreamed of.

CAT. Absolutely! I'm so glad I could be here.

(darkly)

Too bad about *Deborah*.

BRIAN. *(clears his throat, collects himself)* Listen, Cat...there's something I need to talk to you about –

CAT. Good grief. This place looks terrible! Why haven't they kept it up better?

BRIAN. This from a woman who sleeps in a hut.

CAT. I know it's old, but...can it even be fixed up, now?

BRIAN. Evidently not. They say that getting it up to code would cost more than building from scratch. Plus, this sanctuary is too small now. The congregation is growing, and there's no more land here. So the whole church is relocating. It's for the best, I think.

CAT. I suppose. But it's kind of sad. So much has happened here for the Bower family. All those Sunday services, vacation Bible school, youth group...

(a pause)

And Mom and Dad got married here. Even Grandma and Grandpa!

BRIAN. Cat, Please. Don't go getting all misty-eyed around Mom over the building being torn down, okay? She's having a hard enough time just dealing with the wedding.

CAT. Is she really upset? About Deb not coming?

BRIAN. Well...

CAT. I still can't *believe* she'd rather close some stupid business deal than be at her own baby sister's wedding! That just shows you where her priorities are. It's all about the business, the money, the success, *looking important* to everybody else –

BRIAN. Cat –

CAT. I mean, I know the woman is shallow, but I didn't think she'd stick it to Jenna like that. She loves Jenna! And yet she just has to be in Lima, Peru on this of all weekends? I've *been* in Lima, Peru, and I can tell you, there's no business there Deb's company couldn't live without!

BRIAN. Cat, I need to –

CAT. Now I'll admit, when you told me she wasn't coming I was happy about it – you know how much I wanted to be here, and this is the only way that could have happened. So selfishly, I'm glad – but when I think of how Jenna must feel...

BRIAN. Deb will be here any minute.

CAT. *(not listening)* I mean, at least I could have given Jenna a plausible excuse. She would have understood if I'd told her I had typhoid or something, but –

*(She stops as **BRIAN**'s words penetrate.)*

What did you say?

BRIAN. I said that Deb will be here any minute.

(He winces in expectation.)

CAT. *(slowly, deliberately)* She changed her plans?

BRIAN. No. She was always coming. I lied to you to get you here.

CAT. *(still calm)* So, Deb is coming, even though she knows *I'm* going to be here?

BRIAN. Well...you see...

CAT. *(explodes)* BRIAN!!!

BRIAN. Now, listen –

CAT. You lied to her, too? She doesn't know?!

BRIAN. Well, I always did try to treat you two equally...

CAT. Siwezi kusema hiyo ndani ya kanisa!!!*

BRIAN. What does all that mean?

CAT. I can't say it in a church!

BRIAN. What? God doesn't know Swahili? Please, Cat. Listen to me. Six years of this nonsense has been long enough, and you both know it. It's got to end, now. For Jenna's sake.

(*He pauses;* **CAT** *appears to weaken.*)

Can't you just tell Deb you're sorry?

CAT. (*furious again*) *Me?* Tell *her* I'm sorry?!

BRIAN. Yes! Don't you think you owe her that?

CAT. You have no idea what really –

(*She breaks off.*)

BRIAN. What? What don't I know? Cat?

(**CAT** *does not answer. A door creaks, and* **CAT** *jumps, startled. She looks toward SL, throws a murderous glance at* **BRIAN**, *and takes off toward RE at a run.*)

BRIAN. Cat! *Don't leave!* Do you hear me? Just give us a couple minutes, and then you can come back...

(**CAT** *exits RE. After a beat,* **DEB** *walks in SL.* **BRIAN** *quickly puts on a smile and whirls to face her.*)

BRIAN. Deborah!

DEB. Hey, Brian.

(**DEB** *and* **BRIAN** *embrace, but unlike the bear hug* **CAT** *has delivered,* **DEB** *dispatches the action briskly and efficiently, with little real emotion. She looks around critically.*)

DEB. Shew! This place gets more pathetic all the time. When are the bulldozers coming?

(**DEB** *does not wait for an answer, but starts as her cell phone rings/vibrates. She pulls it out of her pocket and*

---

* Pronounced *See-way'-zee Koo-say'-ma Ee'-yo Ndah'-nee Yah Kuh-nee'-suh*; literal Swahili translation: "I can't say it in a church."

looks at the screen.)

Sorry, gotta take this. Give me two?

(into the phone)

Yeah, it's Deb. What have you got for me?

(a pause)

No that's not good enough. Tell them no.

(pause)

I don't care. We'll walk if we have to.

(pause)

Just do it!

(She closes with phone with snap and returns it to her pocket. Then, to **BRIAN***)*

Staff. Some people never learn. Compromise is for the weak, brother dear. Remember that.

BRIAN. Always.

DEB. *(looks at her watch)* So, what did you want to talk to me about? I don't have much time, I need to check my email again before the dinner. Is everything okay with Jenna?

BRIAN. Oh, Jenna's great. Glowing, in fact. She and Scott are deliriously happy – they're perfect for each other.

DEB. Yes, I thought so, too. Nice guy. Not the most ambitious man in the world, but Jenna can help make up for that.

BRIAN. There *are* more important things than a big salary, you know.

DEB. Oh, of course. Stock options are critical.

BRIAN. *(pauses, then tries another tack)* I'm really glad you're here, Deb. It means a lot to Jenna.

DEB. Why wouldn't I be here? It's not like *I'm* the one swinging around in the jungle, picking fleas off the other orangutans.

BRIAN. Cat doesn't live in the jungle. She works at a medical mission in Kenya, helping educate people about HIV.

DEB. Whatever. The point is, I'm here for our baby sister – and she's not. Now, what did you want to talk to me about?

BRIAN. I want to talk to you about Cat.

DEB. *(whirls around, heads back toward stage left)* I'll see you at the dinner, Brian.

BRIAN. *(blocks her exit)* You have to talk about it sometime.

DEB. No. I don't.

BRIAN. She's sorry, Deb. Really, she is.

DEB. I don't hear *her* talking.

BRIAN. How can you when you won't even see her?

DEB. She comes to me on her knees…we'll talk. Until then, I have no sister.

BRIAN. What about Jenna?

DEB. Oh, don't be ridiculous! That's different.

BRIAN. The one wedding present Jenna wants most is for you and Cat to make peace with one another. Did you know that?

DEB. Well, it's a little bit late for that now, isn't it? Cat's not here. Too bad.

BRIAN. She's out in the narthex.

DEB. *(explodes) What?!!!*

BRIAN. Well you see, I…

(He looks into her blazing eyes, reconsiders.)

It turns out she could make it, after all. You know, last minute thing.

DEB. *(aggressively, in his face)* And you didn't *tell* me?!!

BRIAN. *(leaning backward)* Can't imagine why anyone wouldn't jump to do that.

(DEB *steps away from him, begins to pace.)*

DEB. So, she showed up. After all these years.

(She looks toward the altar.)

They always say, a criminal returns to the scene of the crime!

BRIAN. Deb –

DEB. You think it's easy for me to come back here? After what that wench did to me?

BRIAN. No. We all know how hard it must be for you. But nobody's happy with the way things are now, *including* you, and you know it.

DEB. I'm *ecstatic*.

BRIAN. You're in denial.

DEB. You're wrong.

BRIAN. You're afraid to face her.

*(A pause. **BRIAN**'s taunt has hit its mark.)*

DEB. I am not *afraid* of anything.

BRIAN. Prove it. Give Cat a chance to explain. *Without* walking out on her.

DEB. I don't want an explanation. I want an apology!

BRIAN. How long will you wait for it?

DEB. As long as it takes.

BRIAN. Then STAND STILL.

*(**DEB** folds her arms over her chest. **BRIAN** takes a few steps toward the rear entrance, stops and looks back, then practically runs down the aisle and exits rear entrance. As soon as he is out of sight, **DEB**'s stubborn demeanor vanishes. She breathes out, deflates. She looks around the sanctuary, her eyes lingering on the altar.)*

DEB. *(wistfully)* This was supposed to be where it all came together. Where I married the man I loved, walked off in a shower of birdseed…started a family.

(a long pause)

And now what do I have?

*(**CAT** shrieks as she and **BRIAN** enter rear entrance. **BRIAN** is carrying her over his shoulder; she squirms and struggles as they move down the aisle.)*

CAT. Brian, are you insane? I am NOT ten years old anymore!

BRIAN. Then stop acting like it!

CAT. *Put me down!* You'll give yourself a hernia.

BRIAN. That's better than an ulcer.

> (**BRIAN** *sets* **CAT** *down, placing himself between her and* **DEB**, *who has reverted to her stubborn posture – hands folded, chin high, eyes hard. Once* **CAT** *is on her feet and regains her composure, she spends a long moment looking at* **DEB**, *tentatively.* **BRIAN** *keeps one arm stretched halfway out, ready to grab* **CAT** *again if she bolts. After a moment, he drops it. The women stare at each other for several seconds. Finally, it is* **BRIAN** *who breaks the silence.*)

BRIAN. Allow me. Deb, this is your sister Cat. She's very excited to be here. Cat, this is your sister, Deb. She's absolutely thrilled you could make it. You've both been miserable the last six years because no matter what you say, you love each other, and you want this feud to end. So, now – discuss among yourselves.

(**BRIAN** *takes a step back.*)

CAT. *(after a long pause, stiffly)* Hey, Deb.

(She waits for an answer. None comes.)

I understand you like Scott – you think he's good for Jenna. I'm glad. I haven't met him yet.

DEB. If Jenna's smart, she'll keep you as far away from him as possible.

BRIAN. *(steps forward again, warily)* Deb –

DEB. I only mean that if Jenna actually wants to make it all the way to the ceremony with a *faithful* groom, it would be in her best interest to –

CAT. If their relationship is on solid ground, then neither I nor anybody else has a chance of coming between them!

DEB. That all depends on how hard you try!

CAT. No, it doesn't!

DEB. You don't know anything about men! Their brains aren't in control of their actions!

BRIAN. What? Hey!

CAT. Well, if Mr. Wonderful was so all-fired innocent, why didn't you go ahead and marry him? I wasn't stopping you!

DEB. Yes, you did!!!

BRIAN. *(holding the women apart)* And she's *really* sorry, right, Cat?

CAT. *(considers)* No! I'm *not* sorry! She would have been miserable with that jerk!

DEB. I would not! He *loved* me!

> (**CAT**'s anger dissipates. With her last yell, **DEB** too, seems to tire. They turn their backs on one another.)

BRIAN. Well. Now that we have all this out in the open, let's get past it.

DEB. We are past it.

CAT. *Way* past it.

BRIAN. Oh, obviously!

> *(He takes each sister's arm, pulls them closer together)*

Look, I don't know what it's going to take. I'm tempted to lock you both in the flower room* and let the fur fly till you're bald! But unfortunately, we're on a rather tight schedule this weekend. So here's the deal. No matter how you feel about each other, you both love Jenna, and you both want her to be happy. And she isn't going to *be* happy unless the two of you start acting civil toward one another again. So if you can't feel it... *fake* it!

> (**DEB** *and* **CAT** *consider.*)

CAT. I can do that. I'm an excellent actress.

DEB. *You* are the queen of melodrama. I'm the one who played the lead in *Miracle Worker* and *Bye Bye Birdie*.

> *(to* **BRIAN** *)*

For Jenna, and *only* for Jenna, I'll do it.

> *(to* **CAT***, dripping with sarcasm)*

One loving sister.

---

* Alternately, "bride's room," "coat closet," "janitor's closet," etc.

CAT. *(equally biting, stepping closer)* Make that two.

DEB. Just one big happy, family!

BRIAN. No fighting in front of Jenna?

DEB. Of course not.

BRIAN. Or Mom and Dad?

CAT. Wouldn't dream of it.

BRIAN. And they won't guess you're acting?

DEB. Not *me*.

CAT. *Certainly* not me!

BRIAN. And the first one to tip them off?

DEB. Loses.

CAT. Big time.

(BRIAN considers a moment, then nods).

BRIAN. I'll take it.

(He smiles and extends his arms.)

Group hug!!!

(DEB and CAT glare at him, then simultaneously whirl and stomp away – CAT down the aisle and out rear entrance, DEB across the chancel and out stage left. BRIAN stands watching, arms still out, until they leave. Then he drops his arms, rubs his hands together, and looks up toward the ceiling.)

BRIAN. Okay, so that was a little messy. But I'm not giving up. The weekend is young. And I have them right where I want them.

(He takes a step toward stage left, then looks up again)

You've got my back on this one – right, Lord?

(A buzzing noise sounds; the sanctuary lights flicker and die. BRIAN stands frozen on stage, in semi-darkness.)

BRIAN. I'll take that as a yes!!

(He exits stage left.)

ACT TWO

(The rehearsal dinner has ended; the rehearsal itself is about to start. During the scene change, the church has been decorated somewhat, though it is not yet finished. As the lights come up, **NADINE** *is already onstage, stringing up bows or setting out flowers, singing to herself.* **JENNA**, *distracted and upset, enters rear entrance and rushes up the aisle toward the chancel, giving the new decorations only a cursory glance.)*

NADINE. *(glances at her watch)* Jenna, sweetheart! You're back so early! Everything went all right at the dinner, didn't it?

JENNA. *(near tears)* Oh, Mrs. Appleby! You wouldn't believe! I mean, Mom always used to joke about the curse, but I never really thought –

(She breaks off as her cell phone rings/vibrates. She pulls it out quickly and speaks into it).

Scott? How's your mother?

*(***NADINE** *leans in, all ears.)*

JENNA. It's not broken is it?

(pause)

Just a sprain, then. Thank goodness. I feel so bad. Falling down two flights of steps. And before she even got her cheesecake!

NADINE. *(to no one in particular; ghoulishly)* Two flights? Oh, that's not good. Even Mary Ann Bristlemire was able to stop herself by the time she hit that first landing...

JENNA. *(still speaking into her phone)* Crutches? Are you sure she still wants to come? Maybe she should just go back to the motel and rest.

NADINE. You never know about *internal* injuries.

JENNA. Well, if she's sure. You'll be here soon?

(*pause*)

I miss you, too.

(**JENNA** *hangs up her phone.* **NADINE** *waits expectantly, but* **JENNA** *doesn't notice her.*)

JENNA. (*to herself, with resolve.*) Accidents happen all the time. It means nothing. Everything is going to be fine.

NADINE. Of course it is, dear. You know how I love your mother, but I always did say she was just a *little* bit of an alarmist.

JENNA. (*still not listening*) I don't know why Diane isn't here yet…her plane must have been delayed…but I'm sure she'll call any minute.

(*to Nadine*)

And no matter how green Deb looked after eating the chicken, I really don't think it was the cream sauce.

NADINE. Oh no, no, it wouldn't be. No one's gotten food poisoning at that restaurant for *days* now.

(*A door creaks.*)

JENNA. I think it had something to do with Cat.

(**DICK** *and* **BARBARA** *enter stage left. No sooner have they stepped inside than* **DICK**'s *cell phone rings; he pulls it out of a pocket and speaks into it sotto voce, while a flustered* **BARBARA** *goes immediately to* **JENNA**'s *side.*)

BARBARA. Did you hear anything from Diane yet, honey?

JENNA. No. But Scott just called from the ER. Nothing broken – it's only a sprain. They're coming right over.

BARBARA. Oh, that's a relief. Poor Dolores. She never saw that first step.

NADINE. They never do.

BARBARA. But don't you worry, honey. Deb is feeling much better now – you know I always carry a little of the pink stuff in my purse, just in case – and I'm *sure* Diane and Paul will be here any minute. There is absolutely *nothing* to worry about. Everything else will go 100% perfectly!

(**DICK** *pockets his cell phone and crosses to the women.*)

DICK. Jenna, honey, I'm afraid I've got some bad news.

(**JENNA** *and* **BARBARA**'s *shoulders slump;* **NADINE** *perks up with anticipation.*)

DICK. It's Reverend Stewart. Turns out strawberries weren't the only thing on top of the cheesecake. Apparently, there were a few raspberries mixed in there, too...

BARBARA. Oh no. She's not –

DICK. Allergic.

JENNA. *How* allergic?

DICK. Oh, it's nothing life-threatening. She just...

BARBARA. She just what?

DICK. Well, she's...pretty much covered from head to toe with hives the size of golf balls, but –

JENNA. Oh, no!

BARBARA. She's not coming?

DICK. She won't make it to the rehearsal tonight, but she insists she'll be fine in time for the ceremony tomorrow. So there's *nothing* to worry about!

NADINE. *(pushing her way forward)* Why no, you don't need to worry a bit! I've been coordinating weddings for *years* – why, I can run the rehearsal for you!

JENNA. You can?

BARBARA. You *can?*

NADINE. Why, of course. Nothing to it! I've seen the reverend do it dozens of times. We just have to get everybody together, and...

(She looks around the nearly empty sanctuary.)

There are more people coming, aren't there, dear?

BARBARA. *(Also looks around, worriedly. To* **DICK***)* The girls and Brian were right behind us – they should be here by now.

JENNA. You don't think Deb got sick again!

NADINE. I'm *sure* they didn't get into any sort of accident...

DICK. Will you all stop borrowing trouble?

(JENNA's *cell phone rings/vibrates again. She steps aside to answer it, then pantomimes an earnest conversation.*)

BARBARA. *(to Nadine)* Not one more word!

NADINE. What did *I* say?

(*A door creaks.* BARBARA, NADINE, *and* DICK *all glance toward stage left.*)

DICK. See! There they are. Safe and sound.

(DICK's *line is almost drowned out by the sound of* DEB *and* CAT *arguing loudly offstage stage left.* CAT *and* DEB *then barrel through the door stage left with* BRIAN *between them, his arms outstretched, holding them apart. Immediately upon entering the sanctuary and spying their parents, the sisters change their countenance to sweetness and smiles.* BARBARA *looks toward* JENNA *to see if she noticed, but the bride is still deep in conversation.* BARBARA *moves hastily towards the siblings, with* DICK *behind her.* [DEB, CAT, BRIAN, BARBARA *and* DICK *end up near stage left, while* JENNA *and* NADINE *move gradually closer to stage right, clearing the center aisle and chancel area for the upcoming action.*])

BARBARA. *(to* CAT *and* DEB, *in a harsh whisper)* You two have *got* to behave yourselves! Scott's mother's ankle is sprained, the minister is home in bed with hives, the best man is stuck in a traffic jam on the interstate, and there's still no word from Diane!

DEB. Mother, I am a grown woman and the Vice-President of a multinational corporation. I do *not* need to be told to behave.

CAT. She's right, Mom. She doesn't. You know Deb is perfect in all ways.

(BRIAN *winces; he continues to stand between the two sisters, poised to intercede.*)

DICK. Now, girls…we are in church –

BARBARA. Oh, like that's ever mattered before!

CAT. *(sweetly, fake)* Why mother, whatever do you mean?

BARBARA. I think we all remember the "acolyte incident"…

(The lights fade out to black; ALL characters either freeze in place or leave via the nearest exit as **YOUNG DEB** *and* **YOUNG CAT** *enter rear entrance and stand in the aisle at the rear of the sanctuary. Spots then come up on* **YOUNG DEB** *and* **YOUNG CAT**, *who are wearing acolyte robes and holding candlelighters. An organ prelude plays softly throughout the flashback scene.)*

YOUNG DEB. You're doing it all wrong. You're putting way too much wick out. It's going to burn down to nothing before you even get up there.

YOUNG CAT. It will not! Your wick is too short – that tiny little flame is going to go out with the first puff of wind that hits it.

YOUNG DEB. There is no *wind* in the sanctuary! I have been doing this for a year already. I know exactly how much wick to leave out.

YOUNG CAT. Isn't it time to go?

YOUNG DEB. *(starts, realizing they're late)* Shhhh!!!

*(***YOUNG DEB** *jumps out ahead of* **YOUNG CAT** *and starts walking down the aisle.* **YOUNG CAT** *tries to walk beside her, but* **YOUNG DEB** *cuts her off, insisting on being first.* **YOUNG CAT** *tries again to stay level; this time* **YOUNG DEB** *sprints ahead of her and practically runs to the chancel. As they reach the point where they are supposed to part ways and go to their separate candelabras,* **YOUNG DEB** *realizes that her flame has gone out.* **YOUNG CAT** *scoots past her, smiling broadly, and lights her own candles with a flourish. A mortified* **YOUNG DEB** *isn't sure whether to fake lighting her candles, leave, or just stand there, and starts to do each, then changes her mind. As* **YOUNG CAT** *finishes her own candles and comes back to the center,* **YOUNG DEB** *holds out her candlelighter, hoping for a light. But* **YOUNG CAT** *flounces past her and proceeds to light all* **YOUNG DEB**'s *candles herself.* **YOUNG DEB** *seethes, then rushes to* **YOUNG CAT**'s *candles and starts to snuff them. When* **YOUNG CAT** *notices she rushes over and tries to relight, but* **YOUNG DEB** *manages to snuff* **YOUNG CAT**'s *lighter as well as the candle. In a pique of fury,* **YOUNG CAT** *stamps*

her foot, then reaches out and yanks a handful of **YOUNG DEB***'s hair.* **YOUNG DEB** *shrieks and reaches out to yank* **YOUNG CAT***'s hair, but* **YOUNG CAT** *evades her.)*

YOUNG CAT. *(taunting, yet still in a whisper)* Don't forget, we're in a church!

(**YOUNG DEB** *looks out over the "congregation," momentarily horrified. But her anger then gets the better of her and she raises her lamplighter over her shoulder like a weapon.)*

YOUNG DEB. Then you'd better start praying, sister!

(**YOUNG CAT** *takes off down the aisle in a walking-run, with* **YOUNG DEB** *in hot pursuit. They exit rear entrance and the spots go off. When* **DICK, BARBARA, BRIAN, CAT, DEB, NADINE,** *and* **JENNA** *are in place, the chancel lights come back up.)*

DICK. And some things are better off forgotten.

(**JENNA** *has finished her phone call. She walks toward center.)*

JENNA. *(dispirited)* Mom?

(**BARBARA** *crosses toward* **JENNA** *at center.* **DICK, BRIAN, DEB,** *and* **CAT** *follow.* **NADINE** *eavesdrops as she decorates.)*

BARBARA. What is it, honey?

JENNA. That was Diane. She's still in Houston. The weather's terrible, all the planes are grounded, and the soonest she could get a flight out is tomorrow afternoon.

BARBARA. But that'll be –

JENNA. Too late. She's not going to make it.

(**CAT, BRIAN, DEB, BARBARA** *and* **DICK** *all close around* **JENNA** *in sympathy.)*

BRIAN. I'm so sorry, Jenna.

CAT. So am I. Is there anything we can do? Another friend you want us to call?

DEB. *(pushing forward)* That won't be necessary. I'll be happy to step in as maid of honor!

(**JENNA** *looks uncertainly – and sympathetically – at* **CAT. CAT** *averts her eyes and takes a step away.)*

BARBARA. Well, now, Deborah honey, that's kind of you to offer, but it really should be Jenna's decision –

DEB. What decision? I'm clearly the most qualified person here. I'll pick up a dress tomorrow morning. Jenna, you just tell me what you like and I'll go find it. After all, it's all about you!

JENNA. Um…Thanks, Deb.

DEB. Don't mention it. Now, is it safe to assume we won't be starting for a few?

(She starts off stage left, not waiting for an answer.)

Perfect. Because I really need to make some calls. You know how hard it is on my staff when I'm out of touch – even for a half an hour. They just can't do *anything* without me! Toodles!

(She exits stage left, punching buttons on her phone as she goes.)

JENNA. Cat, I –

CAT. Well, thank goodness that's settled. If there's one thing I hate, it's being asked to parade around a church with a bow on my butt.

(She begins backing down the aisle toward rear entrance, talking as she goes.)

But I'm glad we've got a few minutes, because I…uh, have some, um, Masai meditation I need to do…very therapeutic. Not that I need therapy! I'm doing great! Just happy to be here!

(She exits rear entrance.)

JENNA. *(turning to* **BARBARA***)* Mom?

BRIAN. Don't worry, Jenna. I'll talk to Cat.

(He walks down the aisle and exits rear entrance.)

NADINE. Jenna, dear, now that you're having a different maid of honor, come on back with me and see if you think the bouquet will still work. I made it, well…for someone other than Deborah.

(She takes **JENNA** *by the shoulders and guides her towards stage right.)*

Perhaps we should take out the baby's breath and add, oh, something a little more...*prickly?*

(**JENNA** and **NADINE** *exit stage right.*)

DICK. Don't worry, Barb. Everything will work out. The girls are trying. At least, I think they are.

BARBARA. Oh, please. Neither one of them could ever act her way out of a paper bag!

(She looks out over the sanctuary; becomes wistful.)

But at least they're under the same roof. Even if it is a roof that's about to fall down. *Again.*

DICK. That wasn't the whole roof, honey. It was only a few... *rather large*...chunks of plaster. And it didn't crush the grand piano until *after* we'd said our "I dos."

BARBARA. Well, at least nobody got hurt. Not like at my mother's wedding.

DICK. Now, from everything your father told me, that man recovered just fine. It was only a few bumps and bruises, and he had *no* business trying to climb up on top of that cross and fly!

BARBARA. Drunk as a skunk. And at a wedding!

DICK. A lot of people show up drunk to weddings, Barb.

BARBARA. But, the *minister?!*

DICK. *(throwing an arm around her shoulders)* The ceremonies aren't what's important. Your parents had a very happy life together. And so have we.

BARBARA. Yes, we have. And so much of it has happened right here, in this church.

(She walks away from center, toward SL, admiring sanctuary.)

I just hate to see it go.

DICK. *(follows her)* It's only bricks and mortar, Barb. We'll always have our memories.

BARBARA. Yes, that's true. Christmas pageants. Covered-dish dinners. Confirmations.

(A pause. Then, darkly)

Baptisms.

DICK. The good, the bad…
BARBARA & DICK. …and the ugly.

(The lights go down; **BARBARA** *and* **DICK** *freeze or exit SL.* **YOUNG DEB**, **YOUNG CAT**, *and* **YOUNG BRIAN** *enter SL or SR and position themselves in a line on the chancel steps, in that order from highest step to lowest step. Spots rise to reveal the three teenagers dressed in nice church clothes, appearing to watch an unseen event occurring elsewhere on the chancel.* **ALL** *speak in whispered tones as organ music plays softly in the background.)*

YOUNG CAT. Aw…she's so cute! I love that white dress.

YOUNG DEB. I wore it first. Grandma made it for *my* baptism, you know.

YOUNG BRIAN. Shhhh!!!!

YOUNG CAT. Well, *I* got to name her.

YOUNG DEB. You did not! It was Mom and Dad's decision.

YOUNG CAT. But I came up with the name.

YOUNG DEB. Mom thought of it first.

YOUNG CAT. She did not!

YOUNG DEB. Did too!

YOUNG BRIAN. Knock it off!

*(***YOUNG CAT** *sticks her tongue out at* **YOUNG DEB**. **YOUNG DEB** *stands open-mouthed, in shock, then raises a hand as if to strike her.* **YOUNG BRIAN** *swoops in, grabs* **YOUNG CAT** *around the waist, swings her down a step, then moves in between the two girls.)*

YOUNG BRIAN. (to **YOUNG DEB**) Are you *trying* to get us all grounded? Remember what Mom said – one more screw-up and you can't go to the dance.

*(***YOUNG DEB** *scowls and crosses her arms.)*

YOUNG CAT. I don't see why she wants to go with *Harvey* so much anyway. I hate dances.

YOUNG DEB. You wouldn't if you could get a date.

YOUNG CAT. Oh, I got asked. I just didn't want to go.

YOUNG DEB. You did *not*.

YOUNG CAT. Did too.

YOUNG BRIAN. Shhhh!!!

YOUNG DEB. What guy would ever ask *you*?

YOUNG CAT. Harvey.

YOUNG DEB. He did *not*!

YOUNG CAT. Don't worry! I *said* no. I even suggested he ask you. You know, as a second choice.

(*A livid* **YOUNG DEB** *raises a small beaded purse over her shoulder and swings it toward* **CAT**'s *head. Both* **CAT** *and* **BRIAN** *duck, and the purse goes flying in the direction of the unseen "baptism."* **ALL** *watch, horrified, as we hear a muffled thump, followed by gurgling water, as if a pitcher has tipped over.*)

YOUNG BRIAN. Not the holy water!

(**ALL** *stand suddenly at attention, as if responding to unseen parents.*)

YOUNG DEB. (pointing to **YOUNG CAT**) Cat did it!

(**YOUNG CAT** *considers a moment, goes and retrieves the purse, then slinks back to her place.*)

YOUNG CAT. Sorry, Mom.

YOUNG BRIAN. (*to* **YOUNG CAT**, *baffled*) Why did you do that?

YOUNG CAT. What choice did I have?

YOUNG BRIAN. The truth!

YOUNG CAT. It doesn't matter.

(*They stand watching the baptism another couple seconds, then* **YOUNG BRIAN** *ushers the girls off the chancel and toward the aisle.*)

YOUNG BRIAN. There. Baby's all baptized. Now let's get the heck out of here before something else happens! Quietly now...

(**ALL** *move slowly down the aisle toward rear entrance,* **YOUNG CAT** *and* **YOUNG DEB** *whispering to each other over* **YOUNG BRIAN**'s *shoulder.*)

YOUNG DEB. Did Harvey *really* ask you to the dance?

YOUNG CAT. No.

YOUNG DEB. You're lying.

YOUNG CAT. Okay. Yes.

YOUNG DEB. I don't believe you.

YOUNG CAT. You never do.

YOUNG BRIAN. Don't talk. Walk!

YOUNG DEB. *(to* **YOUNG BRIAN***)* If Harvey *did* ask her first, I'm not going!

YOUNG CAT. Perfect. I'll tell him I've reconsidered.

*(***YOUNG DEB*** makes a rush on* **YOUNG CAT***, but* **YOUNG BRIAN** *holds her back, letting* **YOUNG CAT** *get a few steps ahead.)*

YOUNG BRIAN. Not here!

YOUNG DEB. I can't believe any guy my age would ever look twice at you!

YOUNG CAT. Oh, he wasn't the first one.

YOUNG BRIAN. Cat! Stop it! Not in front of people!

YOUNG DEB. What do you *mean* he wasn't the first one?!

YOUNG CAT. Well, let's see. *First*, there was –

(Ticks off with her fingers.)

YOUNG BRIAN. COMING THROUGH!!!

*(***YOUNG BRIAN** *lunges forward, throws* **YOUNG CAT** *her over his shoulder and rushes with her to exit rear entrance, with* **YOUNG DEB** *following. The spots go out and house lights come back up on* **DICK** *and* **BARB***, in their previous positions.)*

BARBARA. They were just kids, then. Somehow, I always thought they would grow out of it.

DICK. They will.

BARBARA. When? When they start collecting Social Security?

(They look at each other, and a pregnant pause ensues. **BARBARA** *starts to say something, but* **DICK** *interrupts her.)*

DICK. I know what you're thinking, Barb. But we've been all through this. Now is the best time for us to go. The kids will be fine. *All* of them.

BARBARA. I just wonder if this is the right time to make the announcement. I don't want Jenna to feel like we're abandoning her.

DICK. We're not abandoning anybody. It's only a two-year mission. You wanted to wait until Jenna was settled, and we have. But we need to go while we both still have our health.

BARBARA. And before Jenna has any children. I don't want to miss that.

DICK. You won't.

(He throws an affectionate arm around her.)

The kids know I've always wanted to practice medicine in the third world. Cat's found a great position for me, and the need is desperate. We can't back out now.

BARBARA. No, I know that. It is the right thing, for us. I'm sure Brian will be pleased, and Deb probably won't even notice we're gone – as long as we can find a way to check email once in a while. But Jenna...she's just so young...

*(***JENNA*** and ***NADINE*** *emerge stage right.* ***NADINE*** *is holding a cardboard box with various decorations and supplies sticking out of it.)*

JENNA. Mom, Dad, I'm going to go wait for Scott and his parents out front. They might not know where to park.

DICK. I'd better open the door by the ramp, too, if Dolores can't do stairs on that ankle.

NADINE. Oh, dear! The ramp. If anyone's using that door I'd better run out right now and clean up my little mess. I had no idea so many thumbtacks could scoot out so tiny a hole!

*(***NADINE*** *puts several fingers through a hole in the box, looks mildly embarrassed, and begins walking down the aisle toward rear entrance. After a few steps, when she thinks others have stopped looking, she breaks into a frantic run. At rear entrance she nearly collides with*

BRIAN, *entering.* **BRIAN** *walks past her up the aisle, gestures toward the others as if to ask what was up with her, then shakes his head and waves it off.)*

JENNA. *(to Brian)* Did you see Scott out there?

BRIAN. No, not just now.

(He limps a few steps, then stops and picks up a foot.)

Huh! Now how in the world did I get a thumbtack in my shoe?

BARBARA. Oh, Lordy! I'd better go help Nadine!!

*(***BARBARA*** scurries out rear entrance, followed by ***DICK***. ***JENNA*** moves toward ***BRIAN***.)*

JENNA. Did you talk to Cat? Is she okay?

BRIAN. *(with false cheer)* Cat? Oh, of course she is! She's meditating away in one of the Sunday school rooms, happy as a clam. Isn't it wonderful how she and Deb are getting along again?

JENNA. Oh, Brian! How naive do you think I am? They're obviously still at one another's throats!

(She chokes up.)

JENNA. *(continued)* Everything's going wrong, and we haven't even gotten to the rehearsal yet. Maybe mom was right. Maybe Scott and I should have eloped. Maybe a happy, beautiful, peaceful family wedding ceremony is just too much to ask.

(She looks around the sanctuary fondly.)

But I really wanted it to happen here, where we all grew up. Somehow I thought, if Cat and Deb were together again, *here*, that maybe –. Oh, I *am* naïve, aren't I? All I've done is made things worse!

BRIAN. Nothing that's happened has been your fault. And as for bad luck, well…we're just getting it out of the way early. Makes it that much more likely that tomorrow will be perfect!

JENNA. You really think so?

BRIAN. Was I born an optimist?

JENNA. *(kissing him on the cheek)* You were born a great brother. You always did know how to make everything better. Thank you.

(Smiling a goodbye to **BRIAN**, **JENNA** *exits rear entrance.* **BRIAN** *walks to center, his shoulders slumping as if with a heavy weight. A door creaks.)*

BRIAN. *(to himself)* Good old Brian. He can always make things better. No pressure, there.

*(***DEB** *enters stage left.)*

DEB. Talking to yourself again?

BRIAN. I'm the only one who listens.

DEB. Where is everybody? Are we going to get this show on the road, or aren't we?

BRIAN. *(studies her a moment)* Why did you have to do it, Deb?

DEB. Do what?

BRIAN. Make yourself the maid of honor. Even if you don't care about hurting Cat's feelings, you made things really awkward for Jenna.

DEB. No, I didn't! What would have been awkward for Jenna was choosing between the two of us. *I* made it so she didn't have to. Cat's mad at me now, not her.

BRIAN. So…that whole stunt was your idea of smoothing things out?

DEB. Worked like a charm, didn't it?

*(***BRIAN** *drops his head into his hands.)*

DEB. Well, if nothing's happening here, I've got work to do. Page me?

*(***BRIAN** *waves his assent without looking up.* **DEB** *exits stage left.* **CAT** *slips in rear entrance and walks toward* **BRIAN.***)*

CAT. Is she gone?

BRIAN. You can't avoid her forever, Cat.

CAT. Forever, no. But every second is golden!

BRIAN. Deb thought she was doing Jenna a favor. By sparing her the decision.

CAT. Yeah, she would see it like that.

BRIAN. You understand her better than I do, Cat. So why can't you end this?

(CAT does not join BRIAN at center but instead crosses to stage left, craning her neck toward the door as if to make sure that DEB has gone. BRIAN moves toward her, placing them both near stage left.)

CAT. I'm not sure she wants it to end.

BRIAN. That's ridiculous. She loves you. You two didn't fight *all* the time. You were good friends once. Underneath.

CAT. Maybe.

BRIAN. There's no reason that what happened six years ago needs to ruin the rest of your lives. So Deb didn't get married that day. She's happy now! She's rich, she's powerful, she's got people jumping to follow her every whim…she's got everything she's ever wanted.

CAT. *(with surprise)* No she doesn't!

BRIAN. What do you mean?

CAT. You keep saying I understand her better. That's because I don't believe a word she says – and you do. She's not happy, Brian. She's miserable. She always wanted to get married and have kids. And now she's worried that's never going to happen.

BRIAN. *Deb* – wants to be a mother? Now? And ruin her precious waistline? Bake cookies, coach soccer, run the PTA? No way!

CAT. Don't you remember the way she used to be? Before she got so blasted cynical about everything? She was a total romantic!

BRIAN. Oh, please.

CAT. Brian – maybe you don't remember. But I do.

(The house lights fade to black. CAT and BRIAN freeze or exit stage left; YOUNG DEB and YOUNG CAT enter stage left and take their places at center. As spots rise, YOUNG DEB is walking around the altar, admiring the decorations. YOUNG CAT slouches nearby, looking bored. They are dressed for a wedding.)

YOUNG CAT. Is Mom coming?

YOUNG DEB. *(glances off stage left)* In a minute. She's talking to Mrs. Appleby.

YOUNG CAT. Oh, no! About what?

YOUNG DEB. The bake sale.

YOUNG CAT. Ugh!!! The bake sale? Noooo! They'll gab for HOURS!

(She mimics two women in conversation.)

"Well, do you think I should make my appleberry crumbcake?"

"Why, of course! You HAVE to. Why, there's only *one* thing that sells better than your appleberry crumb cake, and that's MY peanut butter breeze cookies! But I just don't know whether I should wrap them up in packages of a dozen…or a half a dozen!"

"Oh, I'm sure people will want a dozen."

"Well, yes, but *some* people might want just one or two…do you think maybe I could even wrap them up *three* at a time? Or…maybe even…each cookie *wrapped separately*?"

"Oh, I don't know about that. We'd better ask the rest of the committee!"

*(In mime, **YOUNG CAT** puts a noose around her own neck, pulls it up, sticks out her tongue, and feigns death.)*

YOUNG DEB. *(laughs out loud)* You're such a headcase.

(Her attention returns to the altar; wistfully:)

Wasn't that the most gorgeous wedding you've ever seen? Melissa looked so beautiful. And they were both so happy. Did you see the way Steven's eyes lit up when he saw her at the back of the church?

YOUNG CAT. Yeah, I guess.

YOUNG DEB. You have *no* sense of romance. My wedding is going to be the biggest, most fabulous ceremony ever held in this old sanctuary. I'm going to marry a spectacularly handsome man, we're going to have four adorable kids, and we're both going to be executives in some major corporation. I'll have an office in my house, and a British nanny, and two dogs, and I'll be so important I'll only have to go into work when I feel like it.

YOUNG CAT. You're going to do all that?

YOUNG DEB. Of course!

YOUNG CAT. I don't think I'll ever get married.

YOUNG DEB. Why not? Don't you want a family?

YOUNG CAT. No. I want…a camel.

YOUNG DEB. You are such a dork! You know you want to be a mother someday.

YOUNG CAT. No. I don't think so.

YOUNG DEB. But how can you not? I mean, that's what life's all about. Having a career is nice, but building a family of your own – having all those special traditions for holidays and birthdays…I just can't imagine living all by myself the rest of my life. What would Christmas be like if you didn't have a family to go home to? I *have* to have at least one daughter, so I can give her my doll collection. Don't you want to see your own kids waiting up for Santa Claus, and buying crayons for school, and doing all the fun things we did when we were little?

YOUNG CAT. Like trying to sell lemonade made with salt?

YOUNG DEB. Yeah! Like that!

YOUNG CAT. Not particularly.

YOUNG DEB. You're no fun.

(**YOUNG BRIAN** *enters rear entrance and walks toward them.*)

YOUNG BRIAN. Is Mom coming, or what?

YOUNG CAT. *(monotone)* She's talking to Mrs. Appleby.

YOUNG BRIAN. Oh, great. About what?

YOUNG CAT. Bake sale.

YOUNG BRIAN. *(groans and crumples in agony)* No!!! Not the bake sale! We'll never get out of here!

YOUNG DEB. Brian wants kids someday. Don't you Brian?

YOUNG BRIAN. What?

YOUNG DEB. When you grow up…you want to get married and have kids, right?

YOUNG BRIAN. Yeah, I guess.

YOUNG DEB. *(to* **YOUNG CAT***)* See!

YOUNG BRIAN. *(pointing a finger to qualify it)* But ONLY if my wife *never* talks about bake sales!

YOUNG CAT. There's nothing *wrong* with wanting a family, I just don't think every woman *needs* to have one.

YOUNG DEB. Well, *I* need to have one. And I'm going to have one. I just have to find the right guy.

*(***YOUNG BRIAN*** straightens suddenly, his eyes glued on an imaginary event stage left.)*

YOUNG BRIAN. Oh, no!

YOUNG DEB. What?

(Her eyes follow **YOUNG BRIAN***'s toward stage left.)*

YOUNG CAT. *(looking same direction)* All four of them! And they're headed straight for Mom and Mrs. Appleby!

ALL. *The Bake Sale Committee!!!*

(They swoon together in agony, falling down as if dead; the spots go out. They exit stage left as **CAT** *and* **BRIAN** *reenter and resume their places. The house lights come back up.)*

BRIAN. Maybe you're right. Maybe Deb really is unhappy.

CAT. And she blames me.

BRIAN. Well, how can we fix it, then?

CAT. *(hesitates briefly)* I don't know.

BRIAN. Yes, you do. You can apologize for throwing yourself at her fiancé in a jealous fit, that's what!

CAT. *(stung)* You really think I would do that?

BRIAN. Are you saying you didn't?

(They are interrupted by **JENNA**, **DICK**, *and* **BARBARA** *entering rear entrance along with* **SCOTT**, *his mother*

[DOLORES] *and father* [JIM]. DOLORES *is on crutches; all trip over each other as they eagerly assist her down front.)*

DOLORES. Oh, stop fussing everyone! I'm perfectly fine.

SCOTT. We just don't want you to fall again, Mom.

JIM. You know how accident prone you are.

DOLORES. Me? Accident prone? That's ridiculous. Anyone could have tripped down those stairs!

JIM. Anyone *could*, but you *did*.

*(*DOLORES *glares at her husband.* DICK *tactfully intercepts, peeling* JIM *away from the crowd and toward stage right, pointing out various structures as they go.)*

DICK. Now, up here, Jim, you can see where we put that addition on…but all the woodwork there, and the windows…those are original. Of course, it's all seen better days. When we did that second addition, money was really tight, you know –

JIM. *(nods with understanding)* Volunteers?

DICK. Well, one of our church members used to work with a contractor, so we thought we could save a little…

JIM. Right, right. What did you do about the building inspector?

DICK. Well, you know, he was a member too…

JIM. Gotcha.

*(*DOLORES *has been settled into a front pew;* BARBARA *fusses over making her comfortable.* JIM *and* DICK*'s conversation turns to pantomime as attention shifts to* JENNA, *who has pulled* SCOTT *aside. The couple whisper in hushed tones.)*

JENNA. Are you sure your mother's going to be okay?

SCOTT. She'll be *fine*. She twists something every other week, really. Clumsiness runs in the genes, I'm afraid. Better not plan on any of our kids being tightrope walkers.

JENNA. No? Well, in that case, I'm sorry – the wedding's off.

SCOTT. *(pulls her close)* You wouldn't dare.

*(Their moment is interrupted by **NADINE**, who bursts through rear entrance in full pastoral regalia, including doctoral stole.)*

NADINE. Break it up there, children! No hanky-panky before the wedding! Not in my parish!

BARBARA. Your *what?* Nadine Appleby, you put those robes back!

NADINE. Do you want realism or not? They were just *hanging* there, after all, collecting dust. Reverend Stewart wouldn't mind.

BARBARA. Shall we call her and ask?

NADINE. Oh, don't be such a party pooper!

*(**NADINE** walks up onto the chancel area and raises her hands in a grand gesture. A door creaks.)*

NADINE. Is everyone present?

*(**DEB** enters stage left.)*

DEB. I am, now. Let's get moving, shall we?

NADINE. *(glares at **DEB**, then abruptly turns "official")* Since I am *in charge* this evening, I would like to welcome everyone to a rehearsal of this most sacred and profoundly moving sacrament, the joining of two souls in a pure and joyful ceremony –

BARBARA. Oh for heaven's sake, Nadine, just tell us where to stand!

NADINE. *Fine.* You want the Vegas version, here we go.

(She claps her hands.)

Groom up front; everyone else to the back!

*(to **DOLORES**)*

Except you, dear. You can stay put.

*(The door creaks. People begin to move as directed by **NADINE**. **PAUL** enters stage left and **DEB**, who is closest to the door, whirls to face him.)*

DEB. Whoever you are, you're late.

PAUL. Whoever you are, you're rude.

BRIAN. *(jumps to intercede)* Hey there! You must be Scott's uncle, Paul, right? I'm Brian, brother of the bride. This is my sister, Deb. So glad you could make it. I hear you hit some traffic on the interstate –

SCOTT. *(moves in and claps **PAUL** on the back)* My best man! Thank goodness you're here. We don't need anyone else AWOL tonight.

PAUL. Who did you lose?

SCOTT. The maid of honor.

DEB. Well, I'm the maid of honor now. All's well that ends well, right?

*(Everyone except **SCOTT** and **NADINE** heads to the back of the sanctuary as **NADINE** continues.)*

NADINE. All right, now. Here we go. Scott, darling, you come in from the front door and stand right there.

(She points and he does so.)

And who are our ushers? Brian…and where's our best man?

*(to **PAUL**)*

You'll have to help too, dear. First you'll bring in the mother of the groom –

*(to **DOLORES**)*

Don't you worry dear, everything will be so lovely the audience will hardly get bored at all waiting for you to hobble all the way down here!

*(**JIM** and **PAUL** walk up front.)*

Yes, okay, now the groom's parents sit.

*(**JIM** sits. Then, to **PAUL**)*

And you come up here, dear.

*(She gestures for **PAUL** to stand beside **SCOTT**; he does so.)*

Now Brian, you bring in the mother of the bride.

*(**BRIAN** walks **BARBARA** in on his arm.)*

Yes, yes, you seat her there, Brian. Wonderful. All right, now....Cat?

(**CAT** *waves eagerly.*)

Oh, you don't have anything important to do, do you? Well, that's fine. You can just seat yourself before we get going, okay?

(**CAT** *crosses her arms over her chest, fuming.* **BRIAN** *hops up to escort her, too.* **CAT** *plucks a flower from an aisle decoration, puts it between her teeth, and pulls* **BRIAN** *into a tango. The two dance down the aisle, finishing at the chancel with a dramatic pose.* **NADINE** *stares daggers, then clears her throat loudly.*)

NADINE. Need I remind you children that this is a SACRED ceremony?

(*An unrepentant* **CAT** *and* **BRIAN** *sit.* **NADINE** *scowls another second, then transforms back to giddy.*)

NADINE. Okay, now this is the fun part! Maid of Honor? It's your turn!

(**DEB** *walks in – all smiles – formal, poised, and very proud of herself. She reaches the altar and goes to stand by* **SCOTT**.)

NADINE. Um...Deborah, dear. You're over here.

(*Plastered smile intact,* **DEB** *flounces over to the spot* **NADINE** *designates.*)

NADINE. All right now! The moment has come! ALL RISE!

(**NADINE** *throws up her hands and takes a step backward. As she does so, she appears to be unsteady on her feet, as if her heel has gone through a hole. She screeches and flails her arms.* **PAUL** *and* **SCOTT** *rush immediately to take her arms and steady her;* **JIM** *is right behind them.* **DEB** *stays in place, still smiling out over the sanctuary, oblivious.* **CAT** *and* **BARBARA** *also stand and move up onto the chancel.* **JENNA** *and* **DICK** *rush forward down the center aisle and join them.* **JIM** *drops to hands and knees, inspecting the floorboards around* **NADINE***'s feet.*)

DICK. What happened?!

SCOTT. There's a hole here!

JIM. The floorboard's rotten clean through!

NADINE. Oh, oh...merciful heavens! My heel just went into nothing!

DICK. Gosh darn that finance committee! I told them way back in '89 those boards needed to be replaced!

BARBARA. *It's the curse!*

BRIAN. Mother! Calm down.

BARBARA. I can't calm down! My heart! It's these palpitations again.

(DICK grabs BARBARA's wrist and takes her pulse. Everyone's attention shifts from NADINE to BARBARA, much to NADINE's annoyance.)

CAT. Mom, you're fine.

NADINE. Yes, for goodness sake, Barbara – you'll never last two years in Africa getting hysterical over next to nothing! What will happen when those nasty cannibals come and you really *do* need to panic?

DICK & CAT. *NADINE!*

(DEB's smile vanishes. She moves to confront DICK and BARBARA. SCOTT locates JENNA and tries to comfort her, while the other men move busily over the stage, testing the floorboards and conferring with each other in hushed tones. DOLORES calls several times to JIM, who ignores her. Finally DOLORES picks up her crutches and hobbles toward the chancel steps.)

DEB. What is she talking about? Who's going to Africa?

DICK. Um….your mother and I are going, honey. We've signed up for a two-year commitment at a medical mission.

DEB. Starting when?!

DICK. Next month.

DEB. Doing what?!

BARBARA. Treating patients, sweetheart. Your know your dad has always wanted to do this, and it's been years since I used my nursing degree. There's such a tremendous need –

DEB. *(to* **DICK***)* But you're a *dermatologist*!

CAT. He's a *doctor*. And they need him.

DEB. And what about what *I* need?! Has anyone ever thought about that?!!

JIM. *(bouncing his weight on the floorboards)* We'd better get off of here – this whole section is going to go!

DOLORES. *(shaking her crutch)* Stop it, Jim! You're going to break it yourself hopping up and down like that!

DEB. No, of course not! No one ever thinks about me! What am I going to have if you leave me too? Brian's married, Jenna's married, the rest of you are halfway around the world – and I won't have any family left... no one! Even the stupid church is falling down!

PAUL. Please, can everyone get off the steps?

(Unable to catch **JIM***'s attention,* **DOLORES** *hobbles up the chancel steps after him.)*

SCOTT. Mom! What are you doing?

BARBARA. Deb honey, we had no idea...

DEB. *(in tears; her voice breaking)* Of course you didn't! You never did understand me at all!

(A low, wood creaking/splintering noise sounds.)

NADINE. Something else is cracking! Get me off of here!!!

*(***NADINE** *flails as if the floor is again giving way beneath her; in desperation she reaches out and grabs whoever is nearest, rendering them equally unbalanced.)*

SCOTT. Mom! Look out!

DOLORES. *(from the lowest position on the steps)* Not the ankle! I have brittle bones!

(All scream and flail, grabbing each other and pitching forward, scrambling to get off the steps. The lights BLACKOUT as the splintering noise rises to a crash and the actors scream and shout – giving the illusion that they have fallen into a heap with **DOLORES** *at the bottom.)*

ACT THREE

(A door creaks; the chancel lights come up. The church is fully decorated, but the "hole" in the chancel floor is covered with a large piece of unstained plywood. **ALL** *characters in the previous scene now sport some sign of injury, such as a bruise or a bandage. [However,* **CAT** *and* **DEB***'s signs of infirmity must be easily removed and replaced.]* **ALL** *characters are dressed for a wedding.)*

*(***DEB*** enters stage left. She looks to see if anyone else is present, then moves to the altar, surveying the decorations with melancholy.)*

DEB. Always a bridesmaid; never a bride.

(She pauses; sighs.)

I *was* a bride. I just didn't get married.

(She looks out over the sanctuary; her eyes begin to tear.)

But I was happy here. This church, my family. They were the center of my world. I felt loved…then.

(Her face darkens.)

Boy, was I stupid.

(A door creaks. **DEB** *starts and collects herself. In a moment* **CAT** *walks in stage left.* **DEB** *looks at her only long enough to see who it is, then turns away. The air is thick with tension.)*

CAT. Jenna here yet?

DEB. I saw her car by the other door. I think she's in the bride's room.

(A long, awkward silence ensues. Finally **CAT** *turns to walk back out. But* **DEB** *suddenly takes a small step toward her.)*

DEB. Cat?

CAT. *(whirls around with a "trademark" gesture)* Yo?

(**CAT** *freezes as the house lights fade and a spot remains on* **DEB** *alone.* **DEB** *turns her head slowly and looks toward the rear entrance of the church.*)

CAT. *(from the darkness)* Deb?

(*The spot on* **DEB** *goes out; another spotlight comes up on* **YOUNG DEB** *as she slams through the rear entrance and moves up the aisle toward the chancel.* **YOUNG BRIAN** *is right behind her.* **DEB** *and* **CAT** *slip offstage through the nearest exits.*)

YOUNG DEB. I am not going down there! I'm not!

YOUNG BRIAN. Why not? What's wrong with you? You love youth group!

YOUNG DEB. Didn't you hear them? They were laughing at me! All of them. It was bad enough at school. I'm never going to be able to face any of them again as long as I live. NEVER.

YOUNG BRIAN. What are you talking about? What happened?

YOUNG DEB. How can you not know? The whole school was talking about it. How stupid Deborah was so colossally stupid she thought stupid Jeff Harrison would invite her to his stupid pool!

YOUNG BRIAN. Okay, wait…Jeff Harrison…dumb rich guy…funky hair…ditzy girls slobbering all over him?

YOUNG DEB. That's him.

YOUNG BRIAN. And he didn't invite you to his pool party?

YOUNG DEB. He didn't have a pool party! He didn't know anything about it. All he knew was that his doorbell rang and there was stupid Deborah, showing up all happy and thrilled to be there, wearing her stupid bathing suit, just like the stupid invitation said!

YOUNG BRIAN. Only, he didn't send any invitation.

YOUNG DEB. He didn't even know who I was! Lisa James sent it. She and her stupid popular friends were all hiding in the bushes by his driveway, just waiting for me to show up so they could laugh at me.

YOUNG BRIAN. Ouch.

YOUNG DEB. I should have known she was behind it. The invitation was typed. What guy takes typing?

YOUNG BRIAN. But why would Lisa do that to you?

YOUNG DEB. Why? Why? Because she's hated me ever since, like, third grade! That's why!

(*pause*)

All those girls hate me.

YOUNG BRIAN. (*throwing an arm around her, awkwardly*) I'm sorry, Deb. But, it'll all blow over soon.

YOUNG DEB. (*teary*) No, it won't!

(**YOUNG CAT** *bursts in rear entrance and comes forward to join them.*).

YOUNG CAT. (*happy, bouncy*) Hey, come on back down! They're starting the murder game!

(**YOUNG DEB** *looks at her with a snarl.*)

YOUNG BRIAN. I don't think Deb's in the mood for games.

YOUNG CAT. You're not still worried about that thing with Jeff Harrison, are you? Because that's so old news. Everybody's been talking about what happened to Lisa!

YOUNG DEB. What happened to Lisa?

YOUNG CAT. Jason broke up with her.

YOUNG DEB. Star-of-the-football-team Jason? Why?

YOUNG CAT. Seems he found this letter she was typing to one of her friends. She must have got careless and dropped it.

YOUNG DEB. What did she write?

YOUNG CAT. Oh, just how gorgeous she thought Franklin High's quarterback was, and how she wished she could date him on the side!

(**YOUNG DEB** *and* **YOUNG BRIAN** *snicker.*)

YOUNG BRIAN. Awesome! The perfect revenge. And Lisa brought it all on herself!

YOUNG CAT. *(quietly, almost under her breath)* She got what was coming to her.

YOUNG BRIAN. *(heading toward rear entrance)* See, Deb. I told you it would all work out. Everyone's forgotten it already. So come on down and have some fun!

(**YOUNG BRIAN** *exits rear entrance.* **DEB** *watches* **CAT** *closely.* **CAT** *turns to follow* **BRIAN**.)

YOUNG DEB. Cat?

YOUNG CAT. *(whirling around with same "trademark" gesture)* Yo?

YOUNG DEB. It was you, wasn't it. You set Lisa up.

(**YOUNG CAT** *says nothing for a moment, then, slyly, raises her hands in the air and pantomimes typing a line on a typewriter and hitting a manual "return."*)

YOUNG CAT. Nobody messes with my sister.

(*The sisters look at each other for a moment, smiling conspiratorially. Then* **YOUNG CAT** *rushes back off toward rear entrance, with* **YOUNG DEB** *following. The spots black out as they exit rear entrance. Once* **CAT** *and* **DEB** *have resumed their places, the house lights come back up.*)

CAT. Deb? What is it?

(**DEB** *snaps out of her reverie and stares at* **CAT**; **DEB** *is struggling with indecision. But when her eyes focus on* **CAT**'s *dress, she gives a start of recognition and shakes with fury.*)

DEB. Couldn't you at least have gotten a new dress?!

CAT. This is the only formal I have!

DEB. Get out!!

(**CAT** *turns with a flounce and slams out stage left.* **DEB** *heads toward rear entrance, stomping down the aisle. Just as she is about to reach the exit,* **PAUL** *enters rear entrance, moving the opposite direction.*)

DEB. *(to* **PAUL***)* Get out of my way!!!

(**PAUL** *doesn't flinch. Instead, he stops and folds his arms over his chest, his voice playful.*)

PAUL. Why don't *you* get out of *my* way?

(*A livid* **DEB** *barrels toward* **PAUL** *in a game of chicken, expecting him to move. He does not, and she bangs right into him. She shrieks, then moves around him and stomps out rear entrance. A door creaks.* **PAUL** *watches her over his shoulder, smiling, then heads forward again.* **SCOTT** *enters stage left; he and* **PAUL** *meet at center.*)

PAUL. So, how are you holding up, my man? Better than you look, I hope.

SCOTT. Nothing wrong with me. As long as Jenna and I wind up married at the end of all this – I'm happy!

PAUL. How's your mom? Is she going to make it?

SCOTT. We're not sure.

(**BARBARA** *and* **DICK** *enter rear entrance.* **BARBARA** *rushes up to the chancel;* **DICK** *trails behind.*)

BARBARA. (*gesturing to plywood*) Oh, for goodness' sake, how tacky!

DICK. Barb, honey, nobody's going to see it from out in the pews. They'll all be looking at Jenna. What matters is that it's good and sturdy.

BARBARA. But couldn't we stain it?!

DICK. There's no time now – besides, the whole place would smell like wood stain.

BARBARA. Oh, but it has to be perfect!

SCOTT. I'm sure it will be fine, Mrs. Bower.

BARBARA. (*just noticing him, sweetly*) Call me Barb, dear.

(*back to panic*)

And no, it won't!

DICK. Sweetheart, you've got to calm down. Didn't Jenna say the same thing?

BARBARA. Jenna is being an absolute angel about all of this. But I know she's terribly upset. About the curse, I mean – not our going to Africa. She took that so bravely, didn't she?

SCOTT. She's happy for you.

BARBARA. Really?

SCOTT. Really.

BARBARA. I hope she's not just putting on an act for my sake. Do you think she is, Dick? And who would have guessed that Deborah would have such a fit? I don't know what's gotten into her! Refusing to answer her phone all night –

(looks around, gasps)

Oh heavens, where is Deborah? She should have been here an hour ago!

(to **DICK***)*

Do you think she left the country?!

PAUL. *(points to rear entrance)* I just saw her – she went through that door.

BARBARA. OH! I've got to find her! She's got the "something borrowed!"

*(***BARBARA** *scuttles down the aisle toward rear entrance, but midway there she stops, whirls around, and gestures frantically to* **PAUL** *and* **SCOTT***.)*

BARBARA. And stain that board!!

(A door creaks. **BARBARA** *exits rear entrance.)*

DICK. *(to* **PAUL** *and* **SCOTT***)* Don't stain the board.

*(***BRIAN** *enters stage left. He looks toward rear entrance where* **BARBARA** *has just exited.)*

BRIAN. Hey, guys...Dad. Did I just hear Mom screaming about something?

DICK. Do you have ears? I offered her something to quiet her nerves a bit, but you know how she is; she won't take it.

BRIAN. How's Jenna doing?

DICK. Physically, just fine. She got off the easiest of any of us, I believe. But she'd feel a whole lot better if your mother would calm down.

SCOTT. Maybe I should go and see her…

DICK. Oh, Lord; no, son. One more broken bad-luck taboo, and we won't get mother or daughter down the aisle!

(PAUL throws an arm around SCOTT's shoulders and propels him toward rear entrance.)

PAUL. Come on, Scott. Let's take a walk before the guests start coming. I'll buy you your last cup of coffee as a free man.

(PAUL and SCOTT walk down the aisle towards rear entrance. Midway down PAUL hops a few steps, then stops, reaches down, and pulls something out of his shoe.)

PAUL. Huh. What do you know. A thumbtack.

DICK. Nadine!

(DICK takes off after PAUL and SCOTT; the three men exit rear entrance, leaving BRIAN alone at center. He looks at his watch, then up towards the ceiling as he begins his monologue.)

BRIAN. Okay, Lord, so things aren't exactly proceeding as planned. But I'm not a quitter; you know that. And there's still time.

(glances at watch again)

A little bit of time. I just need to know what…direction to go next, you know?

(A door creaks.)

BRIAN. *(gestures toward the stage left door)* And the answer is…

(CAT enters tentatively stage left, looks around. When she sees only BRIAN she seems relieved, but also tired; beaten.)

CAT. I'm not late, am I?

BRIAN. I think you're right on time. Come, sit with me.

(BRIAN leads CAT to a chair/bench on the chancel. She sits, but he remains standing beside her, looming.)

CAT. You're not sitting.

BRIAN. I need the psychological advantage. Now talk.

CAT. About what?

BRIAN. The same thing I always ask you to talk about. What happened at Deb's wedding.

(**CAT** *rolls her eyes and tries to rise;* **BRIAN** *pushes her back down.*)

BRIAN. You asked me last night if I believe that you intentionally went after your sister's fiancé because you were jealous. Well, the answer is no. I don't. So enlighten me. What really happened?

(**CAT** *offers a stony stare.*)

BRIAN. Aha! I knew it!

CAT. What?

BRIAN. You look exactly like you did that day in church when Jenna got baptized. You took the blame for something that wasn't your fault – and you *enjoyed* it.

CAT. So you're a shrink now?

BRIAN. Yes, I am. And you have a martyr complex. You always have. It gives you a thrill to risk your own hide to protect somebody else, doesn't it? Your whole life is one big sacrifice for the masses!

CAT. Would you prefer I did nails at the mall?

BRIAN. Why did you do it, Cat? Why did you stop Deb's wedding?

(badgering)

What have you been hiding all this time? What did you know about Kevin? You want to really help somebody, Cat? You want to save the day? Then help Jenna – tell me the truth.

CAT. I don't –

BRIAN. You don't want to protect Jenna?

CAT. Of course I do!

BRIAN. Then stop being so blasted selfish!

(**CAT** *opens her mouth to reply, then shuts it. At last she capitulates.*)

CAT. It's complicated.

BRIAN. We've got 10 minutes. Shoot.

(*Reluctantly,* **CAT** *rises, then gestures toward the far side of the altar.*)

CAT. It happened over there.

BRIAN. What happened?

CAT. Kevin-The-Perfect's moment of reckoning.

(*a beat*)

And mine.

BRIAN. Keep going.

CAT. I was really tired that day. My flights got all screwed up – I hadn't slept in a day and a half. So, I stretched out in the choir loft. Just for a second, I thought. But apparently I fell asleep. The next thing I knew, I could hear him talking.

(*Lights on the chancel area go black.* **CAT** *removes any bandages and hands them off to Brian, slips into the choir loft, and lies down out of sight.* **BRIAN** *exits stage left or conceals himself stage right. Spots rise on* **KEVIN**, *who enters rear entrance. He is handsome, but a bit smarmy. He proceeds down the aisle, appraising the sanctuary.*)

KEVIN. This place is *such* a dump. I can't believe Little Miss Sophisticated wanted to do this here.

(**KEVIN** *makes his way to the altar, brushes something from a sleeve, and smooths/fluffs his hair. His cell phone rings/vibrates, and he whips it out of his pocket.*)

KEVIN. Yello! You have reached *the groom*.

(*gives a guilty start; looks around sanctuary*)

I told you not to call me this week! The wedding's about to start! I'll call when you we get back from Aruba.

(*pause*)

I know, I'll miss you too.

(pause)

Babe, we've been over this. It's the only way.

(pause)

No, I told you she's not attractive to me. You know you're the only woman who gets my motor running.

(A spot hits CAT as she sits up – staring at KEVIN wide-eyed. He turns in her direction and she drops back down. But once he is distracted again, she rises and creeps up on him from behind.)

KEVIN. *(unaware)* Of course I'm miserable about it. Don't you think I'd rather be with you? But somebody's got to keep us in the style to which we've become accustomed, *n'est ce* pas? And it's going perfectly. She has *no* idea.

(pause)

Because I'm *good*, Baby! She thinks I'm crazy about her.

(pause)

It *will* work. Now stop worrying. I won't be "married" forever. You have to trust me, Babe. The money's there for the taking. She doesn't *believe* in pre-nups.

*(**KEVIN**'s chortle is cut short as **CAT** surprises him with a tap on the shoulder. He starts, loses hold of his cell phone, fumbles to retrieve it.)*

KEVIN. Yes, um…thanks for calling, Harold. We'll talk later!

*(He pockets the phone and turns to **CAT**.)*

Hel-lo future sister in law! I didn't hear you come in!

CAT. Obviously.

KEVIN. Um…how long you been standing there?

CAT. Long enough to know you're two-timing my sister.

*(**KEVIN** feigns surprise, but only for a second. Knowing*

he is caught, he shows a brief moment of panic, then collects himself.)

KEVIN. So I suppose you're going to run and tell her what you *think* you heard?

CAT. You suppose correctly.

KEVIN. Well then, go on. Tell her. It doesn't Matter.

CAT. Oh no?

KEVIN. Nope. Because, guess what? She won't believe you. You're the sister who was always jealous of her, always trying to wreck her relationships, steal her boyfriends…

CAT. I did not!

KEVIN. You can take that up with her yourself. My point is – she doesn't trust you. But she loves *me* dearly. If I deny it, who do you think she's going to believe?

(CAT's confident expression fades.)

KEVIN. Ruin whatever relationship you two have left, if you want. But Deborah and I are getting married. Come to think of it, one word from you and she'll be even more determined to marry me!

(A door creaks. CAT hears it, turns her head that direction, gets an idea. She takes KEVIN's hand and turns him to where he is facing away from the door.)

CAT. You're right. And for the record, I am jealous.

(She pulls him in close.)

VERY jealous.

(CAT pulls KEVIN in for a kiss. He shows surprise briefly; but makes no particular effort to resist. By the time DEB enters stage left, dressed in a wedding gown, he is an eager participant.)

DEB. CAT!!!

(CAT and KEVIN part in a flash – KEVIN throwing CAT off so quickly she stumbles. CAT turns her face away and wipes off the kiss with a grimace; KEVIN whirls to face DEB.)

KEVIN. Lemon drop! There you are! Someone snuck up on me in the dark – I thought it was you!

DEB. *(ignores* **KEVIN***, to* **CAT***)* How *could* you?

*(***CAT** *says nothing; backs away.)*

KEVIN. Don't be silly, sweetheart! It was all just a simple misunderstanding –

DEB. *(to* **KEVIN***)* Oh, shut up!

(turns back to **CAT***)*

You just couldn't stand it, could you? You couldn't bear for me to finally be *happy*!

*(***CAT** *flees offstage, stage left.* **DEB** *stares after her.)*

KEVIN. I couldn't do a thing about it, lovey bear. She was on me like a wild animal!

*(***KEVIN** *snarls and raises a "paw."* **DEB** *whirls on him, straightens herself threateningly.)*

KEVIN. You know you're the only woman for me, ever! I love you!

*(***DEB** *advances on him. Cowering, he begins to back down the aisle toward rear entrance.)*

KEVIN. I just couldn't help myself! I'm only a man, you know, not a saint! And your sister, well, she's –

*(***DEB** *growls in fury and charges him – her head lowered like a bull.* **KEVIN** *jumps in fright and then whirls to flee out rear entrance, with* **DEB** *hot on his heels. After* **DEB** *and* **KEVIN** *exit, the lights come back up on* **CAT** *and* **BRIAN***, who have resumed their previous positions.)*

BRIAN. *(head in hands)* Cat, Cat, Cat…

CAT. Well, it worked, didn't it? She called off the wedding. I knew she'd never marry a man who would go after me, even if I did start it. It was the only way.

BRIAN. But once it was over – you could have told her the truth then.

CAT. She wouldn't even talk to me! You know how angry she was.

BRIAN. That's no excuse. You've never been afraid of Deb. *I* am, but you're not. So what stopped you from explaining yourself?

(CAT's face flashes hurt; BRIAN picks up on it.)

BRIAN. You didn't think you'd have to, did you? You thought that once Deb got over the shock, she would realize there had to be a reason. But she didn't, did she? She may not have married him, but she *did* believe his version of events. She believed the best about him, and the worst about her own sister. That had to hurt.

CAT. Maybe. But that's not why I didn't say anything.

BRIAN. Then why?

CAT. Because…she *wanted* to believe him. Don't you realize that Kevin was the only man who ever even told her he loved her?

BRIAN. But he didn't!

CAT. You and I know that, but didn't you hear what Deb said yesterday? Can't you see how insecure she is – underneath all that ego? She *needs* to believe that that money-grubbing, two-timing moron actually loved her!

BRIAN. No. She doesn't. What she needs to know is that *you* love her.

*(A flustered **DICK** pops in rear entrance.)*

DICK. Hey, kids. Is Jenna with you?

BRIAN. No, Dad. She hasn't been through here.

*(**DICK** grimaces, swears silently, and exits rear entrance again just as a door creaks. In a second **SCOTT** enters stage left.)*

SCOTT. Have either of you seen Jenna?

CAT. No. Why? Isn't she in the bride's room with Mom and Deb?

SCOTT. No! Your mother can't find her or Deb!

BRIAN. I'm sure they're together somewhere. You know, sister stuff.

SCOTT. You're probably right. Thanks.

(SCOTT *exits again stage left.* BARBARA *enters rear entrance, carrying a can of soda. Her mannerisms have changed dramatically since her last entrance...her speech is slow and slurred, her motions unsteady, her expression a daze.*)

BARBARA. Hello, kids. Is the bride here?

(BRIAN *and* CAT *look at each other, eyebrows raised, as* BARBARA *approaches the chancel.*)

BRIAN. No, Mom. Are...um...are you okay?

BARBARA. *(laughs)* I'm fine! Don't be silly, Brian.

(She pats him on the back.)

You always were such a worry wart!

(*A door creaks.* CAT *and* BRIAN *exchange another glance, then* CAT *snatches her mother's soda can and surreptitiously sniffs it.* BARBARA *doesn't notice; she is looking aimlessly around the sanctuary.* CAT *hands the can to* BRIAN *with a hard look. He waves it off; sets the can down out of sight.* SCOTT *re-enters again, stage left, just as* DICK *re-enters rear entrance.*)

BARBARA. *(to DICK)* Did you find her, dear?

(DICK *looks at* SCOTT. SCOTT *shakes his head and lifts his hands.*)

DICK. Not yet, honey. We've looked in all the rooms, but – they could be holed up in a bathroom somewhere.

(DEB *barges in rear entrance, dressed in her formal again.*)

DEB. Okay, I'm here. Where's Jenna?

(All stare at DEB blankly for a moment.)

SCOTT. *(to DEB)* You mean she isn't with you?

DEB. No, of course she isn't with me. Why would I ask?

CAT. *(to SCOTT)* I'm sure she's just...collecting her thoughts. Maybe she didn't want to be disturbed.

BARBARA. *(looking under pews, behind flowers...)* Oh! Do you think she's playing hide and seek?

(All look at **BARBARA** *with distress;* **BRIAN** *pulls* **DICK** *off to the side.)*

BRIAN. *(whispered)* About Mom –

DICK. It's all my fault, son. She was just so uptight, I thought she'd thought drive your sister batty. I only slipped her a tiny little bit of sedative – not even a full dose! I never thought she'd react like this!

BRIAN. Um, Dad?

DICK. Yes?

BRIAN. You weren't the only one who was worried. When I ran into mom earlier I kind of…well…spiked her soda.

DICK. *(slaps forehead)* Aw, son!

DEB. *(to no one in particular)* I've been wondering where Jenna was. It's only natural for a bride her age to get cold feet, I guess.

SCOTT. She didn't get cold feet! She wouldn't do that!

*(***BRIAN** *rushes off rear entrance. A door creaks. Everyone except* **SCOTT** *looks toward stage left in anticipation.* **PAUL** *enters stage left and crosses to* **SCOTT**.*)*

PAUL. Well, there's a reason we couldn't find her. She's not in the building. Her car's gone.

BARBARA. *Her car?*

CAT. But where would she have gone?

DICK. Maybe she needed something at the house.

BARBARA. But she had her gown on already!

CAT. That wouldn't stop Jenna if she really wanted something. But what could she have forgotten?

DEB. I have the bracelet she was going to borrow. The ribbon in her bouquet is something blue, and her dress is something new.

(A pause. Then, to **BARBARA***)*

Grandma's necklace! Did you remember to bring it?

BARBARA. *(attempts to clap hand over mouth, but misses)* We forgot.

(BRIAN re-enters rear entrance carrying a Styrofoam cup of coffee to give to BARBARA.)

DICK. Well, why didn't she ask one of us to get it? She didn't need to drive herself!

CAT. It's only a couple miles, Dad. I'm sure she'll be right back.

DEB. But why didn't she tell anybody where she was going? And if she only went home, why she isn't back yet? She's been gone for –

(DEB notes SCOTT's worried expression and cuts herself off. A door creaks. SCOTT's eyes follow everyone else's toward stage left. SCOTT takes a hopeful step in that direction. NADINE enters stage left. She carries another box of odds and ends and a bow is stuck on her backside.)

NADINE. Hello, everybody! Sorry, sorry…I was here at dawn of course, but there are always those two million or so little last-minute things that just pop up no matter how well you plan. Doesn't everything look gorgeous! The time's almost here – guests should be coming any minute!

BARBARA. *(raises coffee cup)* To the guests!!

NADINE. *(drops her box in surprise)* Why, Barbara Jean Bower! Are you – ?

(DICK moves to BARBARA, steadies her.)

DICK. She's fine. We're all a little…uh…confused. Jenna seems to be…

NADINE. Well, I don't blame the girl one bit for being upset. The last thing any bride needs on her wedding day is car trouble!

SCOTT. Car trouble?!

NADINE. *(to DICK)* I told you you should never trust those foreign contraptions.

DICK. Nadine, what exactly did you see?

NADINE. What? Well, Jenna's car, of course. Parked on the shoulder over on 7th street. Isn't that where you left it?

BRIAN. Jenna left alone, Nadine. We thought she was going home for something.

NADINE. Well, she probably did…I mean, the car was on the way from your house to here. I just passed it and thought you'd picked her up…

SCOTT. She wasn't in the car?

NADINE. Well no, dear. No one was.

(an uncomfortable silence)

PAUL. Well, if it wasn't far from the church, maybe she decided to walk the rest of the way.

BARBARA. In her wedding gown?

DEB. I bet she didn't have her phone.

DICK. *(to **NADINE**)* You didn't see her walking this way?

NADINE. Well no…but, I can't say I was looking…

PAUL. *(to **SCOTT**)* I'll get my car and start driving that way. I'm bound to run into her. You just get yourself ready for the wedding – I'll fetch the bride.

*(He claps **SCOTT** on the shoulder and heads out stage left.)*

BARBARA. *(to **DICK**)* You know, Honey. I really don't think this coffee's such a good idea. I'm feeling a bit woozy.

NADINE. *(swoops in; leads **BARBARA** off rear entrance)* No wonder, dear. With all this worrying going on! You just come with me!

*(whispered to **BARBARA**)*

I said you should have a "little nip," not the whole bottle!

BARBARA. But it was so *(hiccup)* good!

*(**BARBARA** stumbles; **DICK** moves to take hold of her other arm and he and **NADINE** move with her down the aisle to exit rear entrance. **BRIAN** studies **CAT** and **DEB**, then approaches **SCOTT** and throws an arm around his shoulders, leading him off stage left.)*

BRIAN. Well, future brother-in-law! Let's walk off some of those pre-wedding jitters, shall we?

(*On his way out,* **BRIAN** *throws a meaningful glance over his shoulder at* **CAT**, *gesturing toward* **DEB**. **CAT** *balks; he repeats the gesture more emphatically.* **BRIAN** *and* **SCOTT** *exit stage left, leaving the sisters alone.* **CAT** *and* **DEB** *stand awkwardly for a moment, not meeting each other's eyes.*)

DEB. Well, at least they're not worried about us.

CAT. Yes, I'd say we pulled it off.

DEB. Well, you know. *Acting.*

(*After another uncomfortable silence,* **CAT** *closes the distance between them.*)

CAT. There's something I need to tell you.

DEB. Well, I should hope so. I've been waiting six years for your apology. So lay it on me!

CAT. I'm not going to apologize! I'm going to tell you why I did it.

(**DEB** *turns her back.*)

CAT. Right before you came into the sanctuary that day, I overheard Kevin talking on his cell phone. He didn't know I was there – I was taking a nap in the choir loft. He was talking to some other woman. It was obvious they were still involved. It was also obvious he wasn't in love with you.

(*a beat*)

Not the way you deserve to be loved.

(**DEB** *blinks, but doesn't turn around.*)

DEB. (*acidly*) And philandering men turn you on?

(**CAT** *backs away, stung. But then, with a glance upward, she balls her fists, takes a breath, and tries again.*)

CAT. When I confronted him, he told me you'd never believe me. That you would marry him anyway. He was right. So I stopped the wedding the only way I could.

(**DEB** *appears affected.*)

CAT. *(earnestly)* I heard you coming, Deb. You know how the vestibule door creaks. I figured –

DEB. I see.

CAT. So if you want to keep on being mad at me – fine. But be mad at me for tricking you, not for trying to steal your fiancé.

(**DEB**'s *eyes are watering. Finally, she laughs a little.*)

DEB. He was a slimy little reptile, wasn't he?

CAT. Say what?

DEB. *(turning to face* **CAT**, *for the first time)* I knew Kevin was a jerk, Cat! I just thought he was the best I could do. I was…fooling myself. I wanted it all so much, you know. A husband. A family of my own. But even though a part of me was relieved to have an excuse to call it off – what you did still hurt. It hurt a lot. I couldn't believe you would do that to me.

CAT. But I *didn't*!

DEB. You could have told me that.

CAT. But I thought –. Oh, never mind what I thought. I'm sorry. You know I would never put *some guy* ahead of my sister.

(a beat)

Or my camel.

(**DEB** *cracks up laughing, and* **CAT** *joins her. They are interrupted by* **BARBARA**, **DICK**, *and* **NADINE**, *who enter RE and move up the aisle, oblivious to what they have interrupted.* **BARBARA** *is still nursing her cup of coffee.*)

DICK. We'd better go downstairs, girls. The first guests are on their way in now.

(**DEB** *and* **CAT** *start to comply, but a door creaks. All look toward stage left.*)

DICK. Oh, I hope that's Paul and Jenna.

(**BRIAN** *and* **SCOTT** *enter. A door creaks again. All are* *up front and watching expectantly as* **PAUL** *enters stage left, alone. He is clearly uncomfortable.)*

PAUL. *(to* **SCOTT***)* I found the car. The radiator overheated.

(a pause)

I didn't see Jenna. I traced the whole route; she wasn't there.

(A pause. A shaky **SCOTT** *moves away from everyone – wandering upstage to lean against the altar. All watch him with concern.)*

BRIAN. She must have gotten a ride, then.

DEB. A ride with who? She wouldn't –

CAT. No. Jenna would never hitch hike! No matter how much of a hurry –

(She breaks off, suddenly unsure.)

BARBARA. Then where is she?

(another pause)

DICK. Well, we'll just have to find her. Brian, you call the police; tell them we may need some help here. Paul, you help me organize the guests. As people arrive we'll have them fan out and search the area.

NADINE. I'll go get the church directory. Lois Turner's husband is retired FBI, and we have some connections in the state police, too.

BARBARA. I can't believe this is happening.

DEB. Don't worry Mom. We'll have plenty of people helping us. You know how this church always pulls together.

BARBARA. Yes. We always do, don't we?

*(***SCOTT***'s eyes have fixed on the back of the church as* ***JENNA*** *enters rear entrance. He jerks to attention, then jumps off the altar and sprints down the aisle, swinging her off her feet in a desperate embrace. The bride's wedding dress is a shambles. It is muddy, torn, and covered with leaves. Her hair is limp around her face and leaves stick out from it every which way. She has one shoe on;*

the other foot is bare. All watch, let out a collective sigh of relief.)

JENNA. It's okay, everybody. I'm fine. I'm sorry if you were worried. It's just that I forgot Grandma's necklace, and I was so worried about bringing on any more bad luck – . It was stupid, I know. I should have sent someone else to get it, but Mom was in no shape to drive and nobody else was around yet –. I figured I'd be back in ten minutes, tops, and I…well, I kind of just wanted to be alone for a while. But the stupid car died, and… well, I couldn't very well parade down the street in my wedding gown could I?

(She gestures to the ruined gown; stops in embarrassment.)

I thought I could take a shortcut.

(to **BRIAN***)*

You know, behind the drug store, along the creek?

(to all)

We used to go that way all the time in high school, but now, there's this stupid fence –. Anyway, I had to go way out of the way, and then there was this crazy little yap dog just going nuts, chasing me all over the place until I ran into this shed –. I finally took my shoe and practically had to beat the thing off to get away from it. And then I tripped and fell, and –.

(She takes a breath. To **SCOTT***)*

Does it really matter? Let's get married.

SCOTT. Let's get married.

BARBARA. But Jenna, honey –

NADINE. No offense, dear, but you're a *disaster*. It will take hours to clean that gown. And your hair –

JENNA. I don't *care* about all that. I don't care about the curse; I don't care about any of it. All the time I was trying to get back here I just thought how silly it all was – worrying so much about the decorations, the cake, the guestbook – whether or not the ceiling would fall down! But none of it matters. Not really. Not even this old sanctuary. It's just a building, after all. It's the people in it that matter. My soon-to-be-husband. My family. And my church family.

(She looks toward rear entrance, as if seeing or hearing guests outside.)

They're the real church. And they're arriving right on time.

(to **SCOTT***)*

We should give them something to celebrate, don't you think?

SCOTT. Absolutely.

*(***PAUL** *comes and leads* **SCOTT** *off stage left as* **DICK**, **BARBARA**, *and* **NADINE** *escort* **JENNA** *out the rear exit.* **BRIAN** *drapes his arms around* **DEB***'s and* **CAT***'s shoulders, pulling them together.)*

BRIAN. Who knew our baby sister was such a wise one? People always did say she took after me.

DEB. She's got more sense than I do, that's for sure.

*(***BRIAN** *and* **CAT** *exchange a look of surprise.)*

DEB. I've been so childish about everything. Mom and Dad leaving –. Like they were doing it just to spite me! I know it will be good for them. I was just angry because, well –. With the church being torn down too, it was like both my families were leaving me. Like there was nothing left.

BRIAN. Untrue, on both counts. Mom and Dad may be farther away, but they'll always love you. We all will. And this church isn't dissolving; it's just moving across town. Half the same, crazy people we grew up with will still be there. With their kids. And their kids' kids.

DEB. Yes. But I live so far away now.

CAT. What? They don't have churches where you live? They have churches where I live, and we can't get running water.

BRIAN. I'm sure you can find a church where you feel at home. *All* churches have a few crazy people!

CAT. There are all kinds of families, Deb.

DEB. Yes. I suppose there are.

(A door creaks. **CAT** *puts an arm around* **DEB***, they begin to move down the aisle toward rear entrance. As* **BRIAN** *watches* **CAT** *and* **DEB** *talking together, he looks up, clasps his hands, and mouths an emphatic "Thank You." Simultaneously,* **PAUL** *enters stage left, passes* **BRIAN** *and heads down the aisle toward rear entrance.)*

CAT. You really should come visit us when Mom and Dad get settled, Deb. It's such a beautiful country. And I'd love for you to meet the kids I work with.

DEB. *You,* work with kids? You *hate* kids!

CAT. I've reformed.

DEB. Does that mean –

*(***PAUL** *has caught up with the women, but cannot get around them, as* **DEB** *stands in his path with her back to him. He stands patiently a moment, waiting to be let through, but* **DEB** *is oblivious.)*

CAT. No... I am *not* getting married. Will you give it up already?

DEB. Never. Even if I have given up on me –

*(***PAUL** *picks* **DEB** *up by the waist and bodily swings her to the side.* **CAT** *steps out of his way and he continues down the aisle and exits rear entrance.)*

DEB. What the –. Can you *believe* that guy? The nerve! Scott is so sweet, and he's so –. I've never met a man who thought he could push me around the same way I push other people around! What kind of gall is that? I mean, usually one good glare from me and men just cower. Every other –.

(She stops, considering. Looks at **CAT***.* **CAT** *smiles, raises her eyebrows.* **DEB** *smiles back a moment. Then she bolts after* **PAUL** *and exits rear entrance at a run.* **CAT** *and*

BRIAN *laugh, then follow* DEB, *exiting rear entrance. The lights go down briefly, then, as organ music begins, the lights come up again.*)

(Jesu, Joy of Man's Desiring *plays full volume on the organ. The* MINISTER *and* SCOTT *enter stage left and take their places on the chancel. The* MINISTER*'s face and hands are covered with huge red spots.* PAUL *enters rear entrance, pushing* DOLORES *in a wheelchair, with both her legs sticking up in casts and her arm in a sling;* JIM *hobbles on crutches beside them.* PAUL *seats them, then goes to stand by* SCOTT. BRIAN *enters rear entrance next with* BARBARA *on his arm. He attempts to hold her steady as she sways and swaggers, greeting the audience with smiles and waves.* CAT *slips in rear entrance but stays standing in the back.* DEB *enters rear entrance and takes a few steps down the aisle, but then stops and looks for* CAT. *Their eyes meet;* DEB *gestures for* CAT *to join her.* CAT *seems incredulous at first, then jumps to* DEB*'s side. They walk forward together, sharing the bouquet. Seeing this,* BRIAN *does not return for* CAT *but instead goes to stand next to* PAUL. DEB *and* CAT *take their places on the chancel.* DEB *throws a flirtatious wave at* PAUL, *who grins and waves back. The music swells, and all the seated actors except* DOLORES *rise as* DICK, JENNA, *and* NADINE *enter rear entrance.* NADINE *is still fussing with* JENNA*'s dress even as* JENNA *and* DICK *take their first few steps down the aisle.* JENNA *is completely disheveled and barefoot, but glowing with happiness. Once* DICK *and* JENNA *reach the chancel,* NADINE *makes her way forward and seats herself on the far side of* BARBARA. DICK *kisses* JENNA *on the cheek, then leaves her and seats himself on the near side of* BARBARA. JENNA *and* SCOTT *walk up the steps and stand before the* MINISTER. JENNA *turns to give her bouquet to* DEB, *sees her and* CAT *together, and pulls them both into a hug.* JENNA *turns back to* SCOTT *and they take each other's hands.* SCOTT *notices a leaf sticking out of her hair and, chuckling, he pulls it out. Struck by the moment,*

SCOTT *and* **JENNA** *cannot help leaning in and stealing an impromptu kiss. The* **MINISTER** *shows surprise, but then is amused. As the music reaches its final four notes, the tempo slows to a crawl. A loud buzzing noise sounds, and the overhead lights flicker. Everyone except* **SCOTT** *and* **JENNA**–*who are still kissing*–*look up at the ceiling fretfully. The organ hits its final note with a flourish as the lights go black.)*

(CURTAIN)

www.ingramcontent.com/pod-product-compliance
Lightning Source LLC
Chambersburg PA
CBHW071841290426
44109CB00017B/1894